MW01107246

IT'S YOUR CHOICE !

"Believe and Have Victory!"

Laura Haywood

WESTBOW
PRESS
A DIVISION OF THOMAS NELSON

Copyright © 2013 Laura Haywood.

All rights reserved. No part of this book may be used or reproduced by any means, graphic, electronic, or mechanical, including photocopying, recording, taping or by any information storage retrieval system without the written permission of the publisher except in the case of brief quotations embodied in critical articles and reviews.

WestBow Press books may be ordered through booksellers or by contacting:

WestBow Press
A Division of Thomas Nelson
1663 Liberty Drive
Bloomington, IN 47403
www.westbowpress.com
1-(866) 928-1240

Because of the dynamic nature of the Internet, any web addresses or links contained in this book may have changed since publication and may no longer be valid. The views expressed in this work are solely those of the author and do not necessarily reflect the views of the publisher, and the publisher hereby disclaims any responsibility for them.

Any people depicted in stock imagery provided by Thinkstock are models, and such images are being used for illustrative purposes only. Certain stock imagery © Thinkstock.

Scripture taken from the Holy Bible King James Version. Red Letter Edition Copyright 1976 by Thomas Nelson, Inc.

New Spirit Filled Life Bible New King James Version. Copyright 2002 by Thomas Nelson, Inc.

New King James Version. Copyright 1982 by Thomas Nelson, Inc. Used by permission. All rights reserved. Copyright page.

Holy Bible New International Version. Copyright 1973, 1978, 1984 by International Bible Society. All Rights Reserved

www.lorihaywood.com

ISBN: 978-1-4497-7935-1 (e)
ISBN: 978-1-4497-7936-8 (sc)
ISBN: 978-1-4497-7937-5 (hc)

Library of Congress Control Number: 2012923606

Printed in the United States of America

WestBow Press rev. date: 2/5/2013

Table of Contents

Dedication and Preface

*I would like to mention the people who have not
only inspired my life, but changed it:*

*Pastor Joel and Yvonne Brooks of Christian Life Center Church
in Kalamazoo, MI. has been our family's pastor for over 20 years.
His impartation of wisdom, encouragement, love and life skills
have relentlessly ministered to me over the years. I'm so thankful for
them, and I consider myself blessed to have them in our lives.*

*Through her life, my mother, Arlene Walman, has shown me that
the love of God never quits or accepts defeat. Her kindness, strength
and tenacious spirit are examples that I will always imitate.*

My beautiful children and grandchildren are my heartbeat in life. I love you.

*The Holy Spirit is my ultimate love and the one who captured my pen
and paper for this book. He led me to start writing after my husband
of 27 years, Allan Haywood, passed away from cancer in 2009. Allan
is now with his first love, Jesus. We miss and love you, Allan.*

*I wrote this book to challenge and inspire you on a
daily base and to ignite change within you.*

*This was written to walk with you every inch of the way and
to encourage you to face the Goliaths in your life.*

*I write this with the hope that you will allow the Holy Spirit
to breathe the breath of life, the Word of God, into you.*

I believe that if you read this with the desire to grow,
then God will impart to you the ability to move forward
and to become all that He has called you to be.

Your dreams will become reality.

I wrote this with the love of the Lord for you and your future.

I went through a very difficult time in my life, and as I allowed
Him to move through me during that time, I grew.

Now, how about you!

It's your choice.

Enjoy and be blessed in His name,

Lori

The Power of Touch

IN THE DAYS WHEN leprosy was spreading, it was an extremely threatening epidemic. Anyone who had it was banished far away from their town or village and told never to come back. The townspeople were commanded not to go near or touch them.

Lepers were rejected by *all mankind*. A life sentence of loneliness weighed heavily on their hearts, and an imaginary sign stamped on their foreheads labeled them "CONDEMNED."

When a house is condemned, officials post a piece of paper on the door for all to see, declaring it, "Condemned." With that one word, the public knows that the house has been abandoned; it is no longer a place of safety, but of harm and desolation.

The house and its property start to decay because no one is allowed to touch it. Without maintenance, it dies from the inside out. The long, cold winters and hot, summer days deteriorate the home. It gradually becomes an empty shell and loses its potential for facilitating people, laughter and love.

Jesus understood that this disease called leprosy was itself not as bad, if you can imagine, as the command that alienated the lepers from society. Ostracism was a death sentence in itself. He knew that people are created with a need to be touched by others. We need to be hugged and patted on the back; we need a handshake and a kiss on the cheek. Without touch from another person, a death process will begin deep inside the heart of a man.

Mark 1:40-41 says, "And there came a leper to him, beseeching him, and kneeling down to him, and saying unto him, If thou wilt, thou canst make me clean. And Jesus, moved with compassion, put forth his hand, and **touched** him, and saith unto him, I will; be thou clean" (KJV, emphasis mine).

Jesus did the unthinkable; He broke out of the box that man had put himself in— the box that said, "Don't or else," the box of fear. With love and compassion, He reached out and touched the unlovely, and His touch of love set that man free.

Jesus could have healed the leper with a single spoken word, but He knew that the man's despair was caused by society's rejection of him and refusal to touch him, so Jesus intentionally chose to heal him through touch.

Sometimes we look at the world the same way society viewed the lepers of Jesus' day. We see worldly people as condemned and stained by sin. Stay away, or they might infect you.

As we go through our days, let's reach out and touch people, shake their hands, pat them on the back, give them a hug or a kiss on the cheek, and watch them shine from the inside out. They will come to life right in front of you.

A SERVANT'S HEART

Let's Pray.

Father, in the name of Jesus, we ask the Holy Spirit to constantly remind us to stop for a moment to give someone the friendly touch of our hands. We want to be like Jesus and reach out to people. We want to be a part of Jesus' ministry. In His name, amen.

Filled with Holiness

YEARS AGO, WHEN MY daughter was a pre-teen, she rode the bus to and from school. Her bus driver listened to music on the radio, and my daughter would always come home singing the latest pop song she had heard on the bus. I was very protective of what she listened to, and I would argue with her about what she was singing or wanted to listen to. (She was our first child, so I was learning, too.) But I quickly realized that my arguing method was not working.

One day, as I was walking out of the house into the garage, I noticed a particular area that I was constantly cleaning. I would no sooner get it cleaned out than it was filled up again with debris of some sort. As I stepped out into the garage, I asked myself, "Why can't I keep this spot clean? As soon as I get this cleaned up, there's something there again."

The Holy Spirit immediately spoke to me. He said, "All empty space will be occupied." As soon as He said this, revelation dawned in my mind like a beam of light.

God reminded me of my daughter's music and revealed that, as human beings, we were created for music. There is a place within us that must be filled with music; if it is not filled with the Lord's music, we will fill it with another kind. Have you ever seen a baby or young child bounce up and down when they hear music? No one teaches them that. When they hear the beat, something in their spirit innately responds, and it brings them instant joy.

The Holy Spirit told me that the last music my daughter hears will occupy that place inside her. I saw what He was telling me to do. That day, I put her tape recorder on the counter (this was before we had CDs), and when she came home from school, I had her Christian music playing. All that night, she sang the songs that were playing when she came home. The music I played pushed the tunes she'd heard on the bus out of her mind. I never had to say another word about it; I just kept that tape recorder there from then on.

The Holy Spirit also showed me that this applies in every area of our adult lives as well. What is the last thing you listened to? Or *who* is the last person you listened to? Our minds, bellies, ears and eyes were created to be filled. All empty space will be occupied!

Genesis 1:28 says, "And God blessed them, and God said unto them, Be fruitful, and multiply, and replenish the earth" (KJV). The Holy Spirit showed me that "multiply" and "replenish" refer to *filling* empty space. He said, "These are commands by God" put into motion through us on Earth.

We are created vessels that will be occupied in every part of our beings by what we watch, listen to and eat. Think about the stomach; it must be filled, either with good food or junk food. Our ears can be filled with good music or bad. Our eyes will either gaze upon good things or bad. Our minds will either seek to learn new things or become content with idleness. It's our choice, but we will be filled with one or the other.

A SERVANT'S HEART

Let's Pray.

Father, we come to You in the name of Jesus. We ask the Holy Spirit to teach us. Your Word says that He is our Teacher, so we ask Him to teach us to discern all that fills us daily. We ask that our eyes, ears, minds and bellies would be filled with things that will bring life, healing and health to our physical bodies as well as our spiritual beings. We are vessels to be filled with Your goodness. We desire to be filled with all that pertains to life and godliness to glorify Your kingdom. In Jesus' name, amen.

The Great Love Affair

OUR RELATIONSHIP WITH OUR Heavenly Father has the potential to be the greatest love affair we could ever experience. We can spend our lifetimes in love.

A love affair is a relationship between two individuals who enjoy each other's presence and company. Their every waking moment is filled with deep joy because they know that they have each other. The two have become one (Genesis 2:24).

The closeness they have developed over time has grown strong like mortar set between the bricks of a fortress; no earthly substance can undermine the strength of that tower (see Psalm 18).

No matter what storms beat against them day in and day out or what rough waters they sail, despite all the forces that seek to destroy them, it all fails. Their love for one another sustains their house like an unsinkable ship in a storm. They know that nothing can come between them or cause them to compromise their love for one another. Not now, not ever.

They wake up together in the morning, and as they open wide their curtains to let the sunlight in, they talk about their plans for the day and watch the sunrays dance in the room. There is not a thought about what kind of house they live in or how much they have. They get excited like a child with a new toy about each other's thoughts and dreams. Each cares even for the simple needs of the other, like whether their coffee needs to be warmed up, as they sit and embrace this moment which they know will pass. Their conversations are filled with encouragement as they achieve their hearts' desires and goals.

Like a man in love, the Lord gave His only Son so that He can have a great love affair with you— a love for a lifetime. He knows that you will endure storms in your life and travel across troubled waters. He wants to take your hand and stand with you through it all, to tell you where to turn and when to stop.

He loves to wake up with you in the morning and talk about your day. His love for you pulsates with every heartbeat, and He longs for you to achieve all of your goals and desires. He encourages you and will give you all the help you need to achieve them. He wants to hear your every thought. He is in love with you and aches to share every moment of your day. His joy is fulfilled in your presence. He laughs and cries with you. He wants to meet even your smallest needs. He may even suggest, "Your coffee is getting a little cold."

The Lord will sing love songs to you and whisper secrets in your ear. Your relationship with Him will have the strength of a mighty fortress. He will never leave you nor forsake you (Hebrews 13:5). Though all Hell may be loosed against you, He will give you the ability to overcome it all. Psalm 18:33 says, "He maketh my feet like hinds' feet, and setteth me upon my high places" (KJV).

You are His bride, and He is your husband. He chose this imagery intentionally because a bride implies newness, and you are new to Him every morning. As sweet as a new bride is to her groom, you are and always will be to your God. Never is He tired of you. You breathe life into His soul with your being.

Revelation 21:9 says that we are "the bride, the Lamb's wife" (KJV). "[N] either death, nor life, nor angels, nor principalities, nor powers, nor things present, nor things to come, Nor height, nor depth, nor any other creature, shall be able to separate us from the love of God, which is in Christ Jesus our Lord" (Romans 8:38, KJV).

I hope that now, when someone asks you about the Lord and what He is like, you can say, "Ours is the greatest love affair of all, and we will be in love with each other for a lifetime."

A SERVANT'S HEART

Let's Pray.

Father, in the name of Jesus, we ask the Holy Spirit to teach us to how have a love affair with our Heavenly Father. Show us how to allow Him to embrace us with His presence. We need Him, and He needs us. Holy Spirit, bring us together in this unity of love. We both want it, and we thank you for this new and continued relationship with Him. In Jesus' name, amen.

Energy Feeds Us

Energy is the most powerful force that exists. If you go to a sales seminar, you'll notice that the keynote speaker brings a certain energy into the room. The underlying focus of the seminar is the energy he creates and releases to others much more than it is the product itself.

The speaker knows that there are people in the room who will tap into his energy. After they leave, they, too, will produce sales that meet the high standards set for them. Others will sit in the same room and notice the energy present, but they will not jump into its flow. So, they will leave with the same energy level that they came in with.

The Holy Spirit is the same way. When you go to church, the pastor or speaker creates a high-energy atmosphere when he speaks the Word of God. This atmosphere allows the presence of the Holy Spirit to enter the room in greater measure.

The people who allow that energy, God's presence, to enter into them will experience change. Those who merely watch and remain emotionally and spiritually closed-off to the spiritual atmosphere will go home unchanged.

It is our responsibility to join in the experience of God's presence that is facilitated by a man or woman of God. We have to step into the flow of His presence, or it will pass us by.

The next time you are in a place where people are trying to enter into His presence, jump in. You will not go home the same as you came.

A SERVANT'S HEART

Let's Pray.

Father, in the name of Jesus, we ask the Holy Spirit to quicken our spirits when someone asks for Your presence. Help us to allow You to come into us and bring change. Tell us when to jump in so that we will go home differently than we came. We need Your change in our lives, in Jesus' name. Amen.

"It's Better to Catch up Than Clean up!"

YEARS AGO, I HEARD a sermon on this phrase, and I have never forgotten it. Even today, I live by it. It helps me to make my decisions daily.

Sometimes when you are trying to make a decision about something, it can feel like time is running short; the day runs out of light before you are ready.

You may be unsure whether the direction you are going will lead you to the finish line. Like a mouse running to and fro through a maze, you are looking for your cheese at the end of the tunnel, your prize. It is uncertain; you might make it through to the end, or you might hit a wall and have to turn back in search of a better path.

When you place a mouse into a maze, it frantically sprints through the corridors as if it was told, "Find your way through this maze as FAST as you can!" However, this approach was not the intent of the maze. The object is simply to see if the mouse can find his way out, regardless of time or speed. It is not a race; it is a test for the mouse.

Like that mouse, we sometimes seem to believe that we must go through life and make crucial decisions about the future as fast as we possibly can. At the end of the tunnel, we can only hope to find our prize: the promises of God.

However, in reality, the Lord put us on this Earth so that we can travel the pathways of our lives with Him, regardless of time or speed. Yes, we have to make many decisions along the way, but His Word says, "Thy word is a lamp unto my feet, and light unto my path" (Psalm 119:105, KJV).

God does not want us sprinting through our lives on survival mode like mice in a maze, hitting walls, turning around, running as fast as we can in the next direction, hoping the new path will work, all the while desperately hoping to find His promises at the end. No. A thousand times, no.

Just like the phrase, "Catching up is better than cleaning up," it is better to slow down, pray, listen and walk the path of your life, obtaining God's promises with *great* patience, instead of having to turn around, back-track and clean up the mess you made trying to force God's Word into existence before its intended time.

You will have the promises of God that you desire, but He would rather have you move slowly and "catch up" than have to "clean up."

God has all the time you need. And time is in His hands, so you can trust His sovereign wisdom. Don't worry; just trustingly move at whatever pace He leads. It is not a race; it is a journey. Enjoy the fullness of time as you grow through your life.

A Servant's Heart

Let's Pray.

Father, in the name of Jesus, we ask the Holy Spirit to help us walk through this life, slowly but steadily obtaining Your promises. Help us to listen to Your voice as You direct us which way to turn and what decisions to make that will bring blessings and fruit to us, to our loved ones and to You. We love You and thank You, in Jesus' name. Amen.

Made in His Perfect Image

WHEN GOD CREATED MAN in the beginning, He created a perfect human. But what does perfect mean? Well, one meaning is, "faithfully reproducing the original; without fault; whole."

Genesis 1 says that God created man in His image, meaning that He faithfully *reproduced the original*— Himself, El Shaddai (v. 26). God reproduced His own image and called it human.

He called the first man "perfect," which also means "whole." God created a reproduction of Himself, and that man was complete, "without fault." Thus, the man He created, Adam, was whole in the image of God.

The Word of God says that "God is love," and "perfect love casteth out fear" (1 John 4:8, 18, KJV). We were made to embody perfect love from head to toe, from the inside out, and to live in total peace such that all of our thoughts work together in harmony like a symphony, every tone artfully placed.

When Satan approached Eve in the Garden of Eden, he sought to trick her with a lie. When she believed his lie and consequently disobeyed God, she and Adam fell away from their Father and became sinful. Their sin **birthed fear** into the once-perfect human spirit.

A horrible rollercoaster of deadly emotions ensued, but in His love, God sent Jesus to the Earth to deliver man from the death that overtook his spirit in the Garden of Eden. Jesus gave His own life as a ransom for our sins (see John 3:16).

When Jesus did this for us, He gave us the opportunity to receive Him into our hearts. Once we do that, we become sinless once again. Oh yes, we return to being the perfect reflections of God's image that He created us to be. We can now have the Spirit of God within us, and He will drive the sinner out and give us a new heart that wholly resembles His. Through Jesus, He restores us our rightful places as His sons and daughters. Now we can approach our Father as whole, sinless, perfect people. Once again, we can be filled with His love, and our souls can know the glorious symphony of His perfect peace.

Aren't you tired of fear and the rollercoaster of life, continually moving, but going nowhere?

Ask the Lord Jesus to come into your heart today, or rededicate your life to Him. He wants only to live inside of you and restore you to your Father. Then He will love and lead you, fill you with peace, and enable you to love Him and others perfectly. It is so simple; just call on His name, and He will be there.

A Servant's Heart

Let's Pray.

Jesus, we ask You to come into our hearts and fill us with Your peace and love. We give our lives to You. Take them, and use us for Your good purpose. We thank You in Jesus' name. Amen.

If you have just prayed that prayer for the first time, I encourage you to find people or a church that will embrace you. God loves you so much, and He wants to take you from here to the next level. We, your fellow believers in Christ, love you, too.

One Step at a Time

HAVE YOU EVER WOKEN up in the morning and immediately thought about all you have to do that day? Or have you laid awake at night, trying to fall asleep while the day to come and all its tasks flood your mind, not allowing you to rest in peace?

Maybe you're overwhelmed with disappointments that have somehow crept into your life like dandelion seeds blown across a lawn in the summer. At first only one dandelion popped up, but by the end of the summer, they have spread into an endless carpet across your yard. Like the dandelion, you may have experienced one disappointment earlier in life, but now they seem to have spread in every direction.

Satan is a walking disappointment; he has nothing to look forward to in the future. When the devil tricked Eve into disobeying God in the Garden of Eden, the Lord spoke his punishment into eternal existence: "upon thy belly shalt thou go" (Genesis 3:14, KJV). He then became the ruler of this world, but only for a time. When that time is up, God will condemn Lucifer to the eternal lake of fire.

As you see, Satan has no future. He now seeks only to convince us that we have no future in the presence of the Father either. He will spend all the time he has deceiving and condemning you and your future. He will take one disappointment, and if any discouragement remains in your heart and mind, he will spread it throughout your life like the seeds of a dandelion. It only takes one weed to start the process.

As you walk through your journey of life, you will encounter disappointment as well as joy. We are living in this world with an outlaw renegade, and we must always know that Satan can bring unpleasant circumstances across our paths. Because we are imperfect, we cannot see all the things that he might set against us. But what we can do is take one step forward at a time, guided by the Word and the Holy Spirit.

God's Word says, "For the Lord God will help me; therefore shall I not be confounded: therefore have I set my face like a flint, and I know that I shall not be ashamed" (Isaiah 50:7, KJV).

Whatever circumstances come into your life, the Lord said that you can do all things through Christ who strengthens you (Philippians 4:13). And not only that, He also said, "for he who comes to God must believe that He is, and that He is a **rewarder** of those who diligently seek Him" (Hebrews 11:6, NKJV, emphasis mine). Know always "that the testing of your faith produces patience" (James 1:3, NKJV). You have a great future, for Jesus said that all things are possible with God (Matthew 19:26). He will "never leave you nor forsake you" (Hebrews 13:5, NKJV).

The great I AM lives in you; He is on your side. He will not show you an overwhelming picture of all that you have to do in your life; He will never put that kind of pressure on you. He alone knows your future. Let Him lead you one step at a time, and then He can and "will give you the desires of your heart" (Psalm 37:4, NIV).

The next time you lie awake in your bed, think about the love, goodness, patience, joy and peace that the Lord has promised to give you, as you patiently walk out each day, one step at a time.

A SERVANT'S HEART

Let's Pray.

Father, in the name of Jesus, we ask the Holy Spirit to speak to us as we take on each day, each hour and each moment. Help us quiet our minds and allow You to fill us with Your thoughts of peace, joy, love and patience. We know that we have a bright future, and it is never too late for us to change, never too late to let You fulfill Your plans for us. We thank You for this in Jesus' name. Amen.

One Voice

H AVE YOU EVER HEARD your name yelled out in a crowd of people? Think about a time when you may have walked through a store and suddenly heard your name being called out at the cash registers. You probably recognized your name, yet perhaps you did not answer. Why not?

If you didn't answer, it was probably because the voice calling your name was unfamiliar. So, your senses told you, "They're not talking to me."

The people close to you say your name daily, like your spouse, children, parents or friends. If you were in that same store or crowd and someone you knew called out your name, you would look towards the sound of the voice and answer. You would know whose voice it was, as if you could see them with your ears. In Revelation, John wrote, "Then I turned to **see the voice** that spoke with me" (v. 1:12, NKJV, emphasis mine).

John recognized the sound of the voice he heard. It doesn't matter where you are; when your name is called by a familiar voice, you turn to see and answer.

Like your family and friends, Jesus wants to be a familiar voice in your life and in your heart. He wants you to be aware of how close He is at all times. He cares about your largest and smallest needs and wants. He wants to help you pick out paint, to take walks with you, and to talk about your day. He wants you to recognize His voice in everything you do. Listen for Him. He may call out your name when you're in a store picking out paint and say, "Are you sure you want that color?"

No matter where you are or how many people surround you, Jesus wants you to hear His voice so clearly that when He calls your name, you will recognize the sound of a familiar voice and follow Him. He said, "My sheep hear My voice, and I know them, and they follow Me" (John 10:27, NKJV).

Jesus is our Shepherd, King, Lord of lords and High Priest. He is watching over you through this journey called life, and He is talking to you every day, all day long. All you need to do is stop and listen to His voice.

Don't turn and follow a stranger's voice. They don't know you, and they cannot meet any of your needs. Jesus is your Caretaker, and oh, what a friend we have in Him!

The next time you hear a familiar voice calling you, stop and listen; it is probably Jesus! Just say, "Here I am!"

A SERVANT'S HEART

Let's Pray.

Holy Spirit, please teach us to hear the voice of our Lord Jesus. Help us to follow the voice of our Shepherd, and let no stranger's voice lead us astray. We ask for this protection in Jesus' name. Amen.

The Fiercest Storms

I HEARD A SONG THIS morning that goes like this: "Through the fiercest storms in life, I can do anything through Christ because He strengthens me."

Ahh, lyrics like this play to the rhythm of the heartbeats of those who are facing battles this morning. Songs like this carry the anointing of the Holy Spirit, as He is sends His message across the airwaves into our souls.

The Lord uniquely ministers to us through music when words cannot express our pain or exhaustion from the waves of lies the enemy has sent against us and our loved ones. When the Holy Spirit sings to you, it is a sweet time when your spirit somehow lets its guard down, though nothing else could penetrate through. The pressure lifts from your shoulders, and your body starts to relax. You begin to breathe deeper, the air flowing in and out like the ebb and flow of a gentle tide. Your heart surrenders to the message being sung, as the Holy Spirit fills you with His presence, His peace, His strength.

That is when the scripture, "I can do all things through Christ who strengthens me" leaps off the pages and breathes life into your spirit (Philippians 4:13, NKJV). Truth becomes a tangible power that enlivens you from the top of your head through your toes; your heart swells, and your spirit grows stronger.

Picture Popeye the Sailor Man, weak and at the end of himself, as Brutus, the bulky, muscular bully, beats him to a pulp. Popeye crawls over to a can of spinach, manages to open it with shaky hands, and gulps down as much as he can. Immediately, the spinach gives him incredible strength. Popeye turns back to Brutus, and (although he is still smaller) demolishes him.

This is what happens when the Holy Spirit revitalizes your spirit through music. He releases supernatural strength within you.

God will give you His vision of the battle you are fighting. However insurmountable the adversity appears, His truth remains: "We are more than conquerors through Him who loved us" (Romans 8:37, NKJV).

You will notice that you are no longer tired. Your whole body, mind and spirit will be refreshed with new energy, renewed strength.

The enemy has not changed. His lies are still there, but in the light of the truth, they seem far less menacing. For you know deep within yourself that, "If God is for us, who can be against us?" (Romans 8:31, NKJV). "[B]ecause He who is in you is greater than he who is in the world" (1 John 4:4, NKJV).

And as you listen to songs that proclaim the truth of Christ in you, you will turn to your enemy, raise your "sword of the Spirit, which is the word of God," and demolish him (Ephesians 6:17, NKJV). You will counter his lies, saying, "The Lord is my rock, and my fortress, and my deliver; my God, my strength, in whom I will trust" (Psalm 18:2, KJV).

And the devil will leave until another time when he thinks that you're weak. That's okay, you can just grab another can of spinach.

A SERVANT'S HEART

Let's Pray.

Father, in the name of Jesus, we ask the Holy Spirit to continually use music to break into our spirits when we have closed ourselves off to everything else. Remind us to reach for music when we feel tired and weak. We ask for Your anointed music to always fill us with Your power, strength and truth. In Jesus' name, amen.

Standing

In his letter to the Ephesians, Paul wrote:

> Finally, my brethren, be strong in the Lord, and in the power of His might.
>
> Put on the whole armour of God, that ye may be able to stand against the wiles of the devil.
>
> For we wrestle not against flesh and blood, but against principalities, against powers, against the rulers of the darkness of this world, against spiritual wickedness in high places.
>
> Wherefore take unto you the whole armour of God, that ye may be able to withstand in the evil day, **and having done all, to stand.**
>
> **Stand therefore, having your loins girt about with truth, and having on the breastplate of righteousness;**

And your feet shod with the preparation of the gospel of peace;

> Above all, taking the shield of faith, wherewith ye shall be able to quench all the fiery darts of the wicked.
>
> And take the helmet of salvation, and the sword of the Spirit, which is the word of God (vv. 10-17, KJV, emphasis mine).

The Word of God clearly implies that we will engage in battle at some point in our lives. On the spiritual battlefield, you only need God's armor to ensure your victory. "[G]irt your loins with truth" means that we must fill ourselves with the Word of God, for it is the truth at the heart of any matter we will face.

For example, if you need healing, you can draw your sword, which is the Word, and seek God's truth concerning healing. It is good to meditate on His promises for your health, lifting up your voice and countering the problem with truth, such as, "Beloved, I wish above all things that thou mayest prosper and be in health, even as thy soul prospereth" (3 John 1:2, KJV). And, "by his wounds you have been healed" (2 Peter 1:24, NIV). There are many, many promises from God about our health.

As people, we tend to talk a lot; we talk to our animals and even our cars. And as Christians, we are to talk to our problems, telling them how big our God is, rather than only telling God how big our problems are.

Like our Father, we are to call "those things which do not exist as though they did" until they do (Romans 4:17, NKJV). Whether your job needs improvement or your marriage needs enrichment, find the promises of God in His Word and speak them over that area of your life daily.

God said, "my word... shall not return unto me void," (Isaiah 55:11, KJV). And "it is impossible for God to lie" (Hebrews 6:18, NIV). If it was impossible for you to lie, and you gave your word to someone who knew you well, they would invariably trust you. How much more are we to trust God? If He said that it is impossible for Him to lie and that He wants you to prosper, then you can take Him at His Word.

After you find His Word on any problem you are facing, use it as your ammunition. Put on your armor and take up your sword, His Word, the answer to the problem, and stand in the face of any battle. No matter what, stand. Take your place and don't move. Psalm 62:6 says, "He only is my rock and my salvation: he is my defense; I shall not be moved" (KJV).

Knowing God's promises doesn't necessarily mean it will be easy; battle never is. But would you rather sit in defeat or stand and shove "the sword of the Spirit, which is the word of God" straight into the lies that conceal your enemy?

You are more than a conqueror through Christ Jesus, and in your weakness, He proves Himself strong (see Romans 8:37 and 2 Corinthians 12:9).

A SERVANT'S HEART

Let's Pray.

Father, in the name of Jesus, we ask You to teach us to effectively engage in warfare, not to be full of apathy, but to fight the good fight of faith. Help us to stand and to grow through any situation. Work mightily in our lives for Your glory and praise. In Jesus' name, Amen.

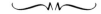

Freedom

FREEDOM IS GLORIOUS! IF it could be weighed, it would be lighter than air. A box the size of the universe could not contain it. Freedom is the greatest power, the greatest energy man will ever discover. Its bounds exceed this life, and it thrives on **love**.

The Word says, "God is love" (1 John 4:8, KJV).

If power is abused, it can cause harm or even death. The same applies to the power of freedom. Electricity brings light and heat into our homes. With the flip of a switch, we have light. But if you touch electricity directly, it can kill you.

Freedom was given to us through Jesus who said, "if the Son sets you free, you will be free indeed" (John 8:36, NIV). However, **freedom isn't free**. Jesus came and gave His life to set us free. He gave us life, and now we are to give others life.

In every mode of service, our troops give their lives to ensure our nation's freedom. We were created to be free, but there is always someone who wants to challenge that way of life. In reality, they are challenging the most powerful force that exists. They are fighting the almighty God Himself. God is love, God is freedom, and God created man to be free.

So, we are fighting a spiritual battle which manifests in the natural world through men. Men fight men for freedom; country challenges country for freedom. The ultimate battle in this life is for freedom, both spiritual and natural.

Jesus is our role model. He paid the price to liberate us by giving His life in our place. In this way alone are we able to receive freedom from the bondage of sin and death.

As Christians, we are to model our lives after His, devoting our lives to bringing the message of freedom to others. That is our mission in this life: to give our lives for others. Jesus said, "Greater love hath no man than this, that a man lay down his life for his friends" (John 15:13, KJV).

Most often, we tend to use our freedom to fulfill our own wants and needs. We think we have the right to use our freedom any way we want, but that is a deception. Freedom wasn't given to us so that we could simply do whatever we please. Let us tell others about our great Savior, of all His power and love, so they, too, may be free.

God Himself paid the price for our freedom. He wants us to live for Him and with Him. He wants to fill us with love, joy and peace. He wants us to give our lives back to Him so that He can bless us all the more, and bless others through us. If we live to give of ourselves, then, and only then, will we be truly free.

His way has the weight of air, and His love fills you with power and energy that cannot be measured.

Your life will be uncontainable!

A Servant's Heart

Let's Pray.

Father, in the name of Jesus, we ask You to reveal what freedom means to You. Show us the price You paid for our freedom, and fill us with the desire to give back to You in love. In Jesus' name, amen.

Friend

WHEN YOU THINK OF a friend, who comes to mind? Maybe your spouse, a close relative or someone you have met along the way in life. A friend is someone with whom you can be yourself and share even the most embarrassing stories because you know they will laugh with you, not at you.

Friendship is an honor to have in your life; when you find a friend, it is as if you have found a hidden treasure, and you embrace the wonderful relationship, knowing that it will last. It doesn't matter if miles come between you, or time is not on your side. Whenever you finally reconnect with one another, it is as if you were never separated.

Your heart cannot place a value on your friendship because its worth is immeasurable. You gladly introduce your friend to anyone, and you are proud to associate yourself with them. If someone insults them, you are quick to defend them. This is what friends are— a covering for each other. The trust of a good friend is a deep bond. You can count on them for help anytime or anywhere; you know they will be there.

If asked to define a close friend, this is how we would probably describe it. We know someone is a friend by the way they treat us and how we treat them.

But not Jesus; His love is deeper than the sea, higher than the highest mountain and far richer than all the treasures on Earth. And His love is entirely selfless. He came to this world and laid down His life for us before we even knew Him.

Even when humanity turned its back on Him, He loved us. He took the sins of this world upon Himself and endured the beatings in our place. He humbly, helplessly faced all evil and darkness alone. When we turned on Him and accused Him, He gave His life. And He did it all for you.

The jeering crowds were a clear sign of their rejection of Him, and the generations that followed act the same way to this day. We are still jeering and pointing fingers at Him, but He keeps right on giving Himself anyway.

He loves you no less. He will share His secrets with you even now. Most of the time He receives nothing in return. He is the subject of jokes, portrayed as poor and very weak. If you call Him your friend, it is because you are weak too.

So, He is a friend with you in a closet. He is hidden in your home. When people mock Him at work or parties, you remain uncomfortably quiet. And He loves you no less.

When people ask you how you get through tough times, He is the last thing you mention. But His strength upholds you every day.

You may be embarrassed or ashamed to introduce Him as your friend. The One who really knows you and laughs with you when you do something silly, who accepts you for all that you are. He sits up with you at night when you're lonely; He cries with you or just listens to your day.

Sometimes the tight schedule of a busy life separates you from Him. For some of us, this can last for years. But as soon as you call, He is there. It doesn't matter how long it has been; He is so glad you called, as if time was never between you.

Judas was one of Jesus' friends. He was one of the twelve disciples who walked with Him for years. They prayed together, lived together, ate together and traveled together. Judas knew Jesus intimately; he knew that Jesus was for him and for all the people. He had never met anyone like Him, and he knew he had found a treasure. But he betrayed Him.

After that, all the disciples ran from Jesus. His friends hid from Him; some acted as if they didn't know Him. They rejected Him. Alone, Jesus faced the darkest day ever endured. He faced Satan, torture, pain and death.

But before Jesus endured the punishment, He had a very brief interaction with Judas. I know what some of us would call a friend who betrayed us when they knew we were innocent. But when Jesus saw Judas, He said, "**Friend**, wherefore art thou come?" (Matthew 26:50, KJV, emphasis mine). Jesus wanted Judas to know, even then, that He had **already** forgiven him. He wanted to let him know how much He still loved him.

Because Jesus was not looking out for Himself, people didn't have to meet certain criteria to be His friends. When you hurt Him, He loves you. If you turn on Him, He loves you. In light of His example, we need to be careful how we define friendship. We need to be in a place where we can give to people without expecting anything in return. Like Jesus, we are to love the unlovely, bless the scornful, and reach out and help others at all times. And then, when they reject you without so much as a, "Thank you," you can look into their eyes and call them "**friend**."

A Servant's Heart

Let's Pray.

Father, in the name of Jesus, help us and teach us to be friends who don't expect anything in return. Teach us to love, to give and then give some more. We want to be free like Jesus. We want to embody His kind of love. In Jesus' name, amen.

Fear

FEAR WAS GIVEN TO us for a healthy purpose. In the Old Testament, fear was a way to describe reverence for the Lord, an unparalleled respect for the Almighty. What the Bible describes as "the fear of the Lord" does not mean that we need to be afraid of Him.

Another healthy form of fear is meant to caution us, like when you get too close to a poisonous snake or a hot flame. This fear protects us from danger. When that emotion surges in the pit of your stomach, your brain is saying, "Stop! This is going to hurt!"

We need fear, but only in its intended form. When fear manifests the wrong way, then the emotion that was meant to protect you can destroy you.

When it gets out of control, this emotion is sometimes called the "spirit of fear." Satan twists what God meant for good and uses the same force against you. He wants to paralyze you so that you cannot fulfill God's great purpose for your life. See, Satan is not a creator; he is merely a fallen angel created by God. But he watched God create man and he knows how God's kingdom works and how to play upon our fears.

So, if fear is not controlled, it will paralyze you and keep you from your destiny. It will prevent you from becoming the person you were created to be. Fear can be such a strong force that it can cause us to run this race called life in place, as if we were on a treadmill. We can grow old and die and never accomplish the true desires of our hearts. Fear may even keep us from ever discovering those desires.

The Word of God says, "God has not given us a spirit of fear, but of power and of love and of a sound mind" (2 Timothy 1:7, NKJV). You can stand up today, turn against this spirit of fear, and tell it to leave you alone in the name of Jesus. Open the Word and read the promises of God that were written to help us stand our ground against the enemy. Speak the Word into the situations that hold you back, whether it is marriage, having children, finding work, buying a house, unused talents or sickness.

Learn to recognize and despise this fear because it was sent to destroy you and your dreams. Don't allow it to control you. You were created to prosper in every area of your life. You can do it.

Sure, it's work. But it is much more difficult to sit in apathy while life passes you by. It is much more exhausting to watch your dreams float by than it is to stand up and take back what is rightfully yours. As the saying goes, "It takes more muscles to frown than it does to smile."

So, what is it going to be? Are you going to choose fear, or will you confidently chase your dreams? Go for it; you can do all things through Christ who strengthens you! (Philippians 4:13).

A Servant's Heart

Let's Pray.

Father, in the name of Jesus, please help us to stand up to the fear in our lives. We ask for Your strength so that we can become all that You have called us to be. Teach us tenacity. Strengthen our hearts. Give us the perseverance to pursue our dreams and the confidence to make good decisions. Don't let us sit on the sideline and watch our dreams go by. We thank You. In Jesus' name, amen.

Hearing

HAVE YOU EVER HEARD your voice played back on a tape recorder? If you're anything like me, it didn't sound like you at all. But why is hearing your own voice played back so different from hearing a recording of someone else's voice, which sounds just like them?

It's because God created you with two sets of ears. We use one set to hear the outside world. I once heard a man describe these as "catchers" because they catch the words that are being said from the outside.

But you also have inner ears, which are made up of a bone structure inside your head. The inner ear feeds your voice directly into your human spirit, which is often referred to as your "heart." When you talk or sing, you hear your own voice with your inner ear, and that is the sound you become familiar with. But when you hear a recording of your voice, you are hearing yourself with your outer ears. That's why it sounds so different.

God created us this way for a reason; He gave us inner ears so that we could build our own faith. The Bible says, "David encouraged himself" (1 Samuel 30:6, KJV). Many times in his life, everyone was against David—even his own family. But he knew the heart of God, and he knew that his voice was the key to building his faith. So King David spoke the truth out loud to encourage himself.

It is nice to have people in our lives who encourage us, but you can't rely on them to carry you through every hardship. They are a **support** system, but they are not meant to be the system's foundation.

In the system God created for us, we are to read His Word aloud and listen to ourselves speak. The Bible says, "faith comes by **hearing,** and **hearing** by the word of God" (Romans 10:17, NKJV, emphasis mine). The more you speak God's truth, the greater your foundation of faith becomes. We are supposed to speak God's promises into the areas of our lives where we desire change.

It's great to have people encourage you from the outside, but it is equally if not more important to hear encouragement from the inside, from your own voice. Your voice speaks directly into your spirit, and it will drive out doubt and replace it with faith.

Jesus said, "Have faith in God. For assuredly, I say to you, whoever **says** to this mountain, 'Be removed and be cast into the sea,' and does not **doubt in his heart**, but believes that those things he **says** will be done, he will have whatever he **says**" (Matthew 11:22-23, NKJV, emphasis mine).

Let's look at this again: Faith comes by hearing God's Word, which is released by speaking the promises of God; then doubt leaves your heart, and your mountain moves.

Jesus didn't say, "Think about the promises of God," or, "Pray in your mind." Nor did He say, "Listen to your favorite minister, and gain faith through them." He said, "Speak, and don't doubt in your heart, and you will have whatever you say."

Faith is the opposite of doubt, and it is built from hearing the Word of God— by hearing your own voice from the inside, speaking the promises of God on a daily basis. When you do this, you are calling "those things which be not as though they were," just as your Father does (Romans 4:17, KJV).

Your own voice is the greatest encourager of all. When it aligns with the Word of God, it is an unstoppable force that will move mountains in your life. Faith that begins as a trickling brook will become the rushing waters of Niagara Falls, strong enough to bring change to any situation. That is why God wants us to lift up our voices to Him and pray, praise and worship aloud at home, in the car, at work, anytime, anywhere. Faith will come, and it will move that mountain.

Don't wait for someone else to build your faith; it won't happen. You have the ability to change your own situation. You have been given four ears: two for listening to others and two for listening to yourself. Now use all four of your "catchers," and watch your mountain move!

A Servant's Heart

Let's Pray.

Father, in the name of Jesus, we ask You to reveal to us the influence of our own voices as we proclaim Your promises daily. Teach us how to move our circumstances in the right direction, and not to rely on others to do it for us. Teach us not to listen to others only, but to build our faith by speaking Your Word and listening to our own voices. We need revelation in these areas of our lives, and we thank You for the truth that lives within us in Jesus' name. Amen.

Images

GOD HAS GIVEN US the gift of creativity. We create images when we paint, when we take photographs, and we also evoke images when we speak. We have this gift from God— the gift of creating images with our words. God said, "Death and life are in the power of the tongue" (Proverbs 18:21, KJV).

Let's use this phrase as an example: *Look at that big, ugly, dirty dog.*

When you read those words, your brain created a mental image, and you can envision the dog. You also may have attached emotions to your mental picture, such as fear or sadness.

Research has discovered that the part of the brain that controls human speech is connected to every nerve of the body. As a result, the words that you speak about yourself can affect your health in a positive or negative way.

Doctors now recognize that emotions have the power to create and release either healthy or damaging hormones into your body. These emotions are a reaction to what you perceive to be true in a situation, but over time they can cause harmful effects, such as heart attacks and sickness.

People have always believed that we should watch what we say, and now we know why this is so important. Words create mental pictures and then release emotions in the form of hormones into every nerve of your body.

If you like to read, you understand this truth well. A good author can create a mental image so powerful that their readers' are moved to tears or laughter. An author can also stir such fear in a reader that they may be afraid to be alone at night. This is true because words create images, which in turn evoke emotions. This process starts in the brain but is released into nerves as well as the human spirit.

God created this as a blessing before man sinned in the Garden of Eden. But Satan interfered and perverted this gift that God intended for good. Now, he uses it against us.

If we are aware of how God created us, then we can focus on using our gifts to help and not harm ourselves. He gives us the power to overcome the evil one, and we are responsible for using it correctly.

Think of the natural gas we use to heat our homes. If used correctly, it will provide heat and comfort through the harsh winter. But if it is used incorrectly, it can cause harm and even death. We have access to natural gas because it can help us, but it comes with the responsibility to use it correctly.

Responsibility always accompanies power. As I have told my children, "Driving a car is so easy, it's dangerous. You have responsibility when you get in the driver's seat." We are the drivers, and our bodies are the cars. God freely gives us good gifts, but we should not recklessly abuse them.

Even if you're not aware of how the system works, it is in effect; your words are powerful. If you don't understand the responsibility of driving a car, and you get in and take off, you could hurt someone. Not being aware of how your body works doesn't change the fact that you're in charge, and there are laws set in motion by God that govern how it works.

It would be a good idea to record yourself speaking for a day or two, and then sit down and listen to it. I think we would all be surprised at what we create and release into our bodies daily.

If your body was a car, and your words reflected how skillfully, carefully or recklessly you drove, would you feel safe in your own vehicle?

Listen to yourself, and ask others to hold you accountable. It takes time to change habits, but they can be changed.

Now that you are aware of your responsibility, drive safely.

A Servant's Heart

Let's Pray.

Holy Spirit, in the name of Jesus, we ask You to teach us the power of our tongues. Your Word says that our tongues can speak death and life, and we choose life. We know that there is much we still need to learn. Teach us, Holy Spirit, to speak blessings into our lives and not to recklessly speak curses upon ourselves. Teach us to embrace our responsibility for our own lives and not to despise the gifts You have given us. In Jesus' name, amen.

I would encourage you to read the Book of Proverbs, starting in Chapter 10. The truth of the power of the tongue lies within these pages.

Under Pressure

THE DICTIONARY DEFINES PRESSURE as, "The burden of physical or mental distress, the constraint of circumstance, the weight of social or economic imposition."

Are you allowing pressure to burden you? Pressure always starts as a little voice in your head. The holiday season provides a great example: "Christmas is coming up, and I still haven't started buying gifts!" or, "I'm not close to my family, so why should I even celebrate this holiday?"

If you continue down this path, by the time the holiday comes, you will be like a balloon filled up with too much air; you could pop at any moment, whenever someone rubs you the wrong way. Then WHAM! You break, and everyone runs.

It doesn't have to be that way. **Pressure can be used to help you**, not break you. I've been taught that pressure reveals weakness.

If an inner tube has a hole in it, and you put it under water and squeeze it, bubbles emerge from the hole. The pressure you put on the inner tube reveals where it is weak. Then you can patch up the tube and float on. The **pressure showed you where the problem was** so that you could focus on fixing that spot.

We are like the inner tube. If we try to ignore our weaknesses, pressure will cause us to break down, and our weaknesses will inevitably show. We may never even know why.

Instead, we should be willing to look within ourselves and ask the Lord, "Why am I feeling this way right now?" or, "Could You show me why I'm feeling so much pressure in this area?"

With His gentle guidance, we will discover that there is a core issue behind the weight that burdens us. If we don't address the core issue, then the weight could become so great that it eventually hurts us or someone we love.

The people around you can usually sense the pressure that weighs on you, and they will probably begin to approach you like they are walking on egg shells. No one feels free to laugh too much or too loud, or they feel like they can't mention someone's name in your presence. Maybe they try to avoid you altogether because they are afraid you might blow.

Perhaps this is not you at all, but you feel pressure in another area. It really doesn't matter what kind of pressure you deal with; it's all bad, and it needs to go— for your sake and the sakes of everyone in your life. Aren't you tired of feeling like you're under pressure? It takes a lot of energy to live that way, year after year.

This year, allow pressure to show you where you are weak. Let this be the year when you become free— free from the weight of daily tasks, from hurt caused by others, and from your own expectations. Work on turning your weaknesses into your strengths.

This might be a painful process because growing is painful. Change can be difficult, but by this time next year, you could be a new person in your area of former weakness, full of strength, joy and peace. You can be free to laugh from a deep place of joy within you, instead of resorting to a shallow, superficial laugh that poorly masks the weight on your shoulders.

Let's be humble enough to recognize our weaknesses when pressure reveals them. Let's go to the Lord this time and ask for His help to let go. Ask Him for His strength; He will give it to you, "for," He said, "my strength is made perfect in weakness" (2 Corinthians 12:9, KJV).

Learn from pressure this year, humbly invite God to bring change, and let yourself grow. And then, when someone reaches out to touch you, you won't pop, and they won't run.

A Servant's Heart

Let's Pray.

Father, in the name of Jesus, we ask You to show us where we need to grow, and how to let go of past hurts. We need You, Lord, and we are asking for all to be revealed to us this year. Help us to allow the pressure we feel to be our teacher. We don't want to stay the same, and we thank You for Your strength that helps us change. In Jesus' name, amen.

The Five Senses

SIGHT, SMELL, TASTE, TOUCH and Hearing— we have been given these abilities to help us communicate with and experience the world. However, we were not intended to rely on those senses alone to experience all that life has to offer.

In the Garden of Eden, the Bible implies that God regularly walked and talked with Adam (see Genesis 3:8-9). Adam interacted with God on a daily basis, and he knew God as his close friend and Father. They probably laughed and guessed each other's thoughts.

Adam did not only use his physical senses to relate to God; he could also hear God approach with his spirit— his inner ears. Adam understood the thoughts of God; he loved God's heart and all of His intents. He also knew that he could trust God with his life. Adam lived completely free from fear. He was not only free from the physical sense of fear, which suddenly rushes in when we see a snake; this kind of fear leaves as quickly as it came. Adam had also never experienced the fear that deeply roots itself in our hearts.

In the Garden, Adam was sensitive to the Lord because he was sinless. Because of his close relationship with God, Adam's experience was governed by his spiritual senses and complimented by his physical ones. This reality directly contrasts our experience after the Fall of Man. In the Garden, to live in a physical body was to walk physically with God, and Adam's faith was based upon his sight. His spirit was in perfect, holy unison with his flesh (as opposed to Paul's words in 2 Corinthians 5:6-7).

The Garden of Eden wasn't merely a location; it was a way of life. The Earth yielded to the commands of man. Hunger was never an issue because food wasn't something they had to labor for. Utopia was a daily reality.

If Adam didn't know which direction to take or what decision to make, he would ask the Lord for wisdom and **wait** for peace. If peace didn't come, then he wouldn't make that decision. He **waited** for God's wisdom, and then moved forward with the plan.

See, Adam and Eve were as alive as we are, but they naturally relied on different senses to live because their spirits were vibrantly alive. They lived in perfect love, joy, peace, longsuffering, gentleness, goodness, faith, meekness and temperance (see Galatians 5:22-23). These are a different type of food called the "fruit of the Spirit," and Adam and Eve could live this way because they were connected to the Tree that produces this fruit— that is, the Tree of Life, who is Jesus.

But after Adam sinned, he was separated from God. It is important to note that Adam changed, not God. God is the same today, yesterday and forever (Hebrews 13:8). And not only was Adam physically separated from God; his inner senses were separated as well. He was no longer able to openly communicate with God because he was separated from the Tree of Life. Mankind had to develop a different way to survive, and that's when we became entirely dependent upon our five physical senses.

When you connect with Jesus, you begin drawing from the same Tree that flourished in the Garden. Your spirit will be restored, and you can rely on the fruit of the Spirit to make a living. You'll be like Adam, restored.

The Earth **will** yield fruit and not thorns. Fear will submit to peace. Love will replace anger. Perseverance will run out weakness. Wisdom will overcome foolishness. Ecstasy and utopia will be a daily reality.

You won't have to rely on partying or any kind of overindulgence to get that feeling. You won't rely solely on your sight, hearing, smell, taste or touch to make decisions. "For," the Word says, "we walk by faith, not by sight" (2 Corinthians 5:7, KJV).

Now you can live and trust your senses because they are connected to "the way, the truth, and the life" (John 14:6, KJV).

A SERVANT'S HEART

Let's Pray.

Father, in the name of Jesus, we ask You to teach us to develop our spiritual senses, the fruits of the Spirit. We want to live the abundant lives that Jesus came to give us (John 10:10). We want to eat from the Tree of Life. We want to live in utopia with You in the midst of this imperfect world, and we know that Your Holy Spirit holds the key to that joy and peace. We seek You for this, Lord, in Jesus' name. Amen.

Fair

HAVE YOU EVER THOUGHT that life is unfair? As children, we were raised with a thought process that can hurt us as adults. We assume that will be smooth-sailing with no troubled waters. And when the waters prove to be plenty troublesome, we fall into thinking, "Life isn't fair."

What does the word "fair" mean to you? Let's take a look at the dictionary's definition: "Marked by impartiality and honesty: free from self-interest, prejudice, or favoritism" (Webster's?).

The Word of God says, "God is no respecter of persons" (Acts 10:34, KJV). And His Word does not return to Him void (Isaiah 55:11).

God is the most fair of all because He does not favor anyone above anyone else. He equally favors all who know Jesus, for we are all sons and daughters of God (1 John 3:1). But that doesn't necessarily fall into what we would deem, "fair."

We sometimes believe that all men are equal, and that is fair. This is not true! Look at Tiger Woods. He has been given the talent to play an amazing game of golf, better than nearly every player before him. Yes, he spent years developing his gift, but so have others, and they don't seem to have the same potential as Tiger Woods. The same was true of great singers like Michael Jackson and Elvis Presley. They were gifted in an arena of their own. No matter how many years I spend in voice lessons, I will be no Michael Jackson because we are not equal.

Some of us are born into poverty and war, others into blessing and freedom. Is that fair? Is that equal?

Yes, in the kingdom of God, it is both. When God created mankind in the Garden of Eden, He gave **all** of us complete dominion over the Earth. We had it made. But because of the rebellion of mankind, we lost it all. **We gave** ownership of the Earth over to Satan.

Satan played a game with us; we disobeyed God, and he won. He won, but only for a time!

So yes, it was fair alright.

Now we are dealing with the cost of sin. The Earth is in a mess, and it just keeps getting messier. But the good news is, Jesus stepped in. He came to the Earth, and He won it back, giving mankind back our salvation. Satan lost, and it is forever fair.

We are now restored to the position of the original Adam. Once again, we have power and dominion over the Earth, and again we are the sons and daughters of God.

But we are still dealing with the repercussions of Adam's sin, as we finish out this Earth's time of existence. When that time is up, God will send the Bridegroom. Jesus will come back to this world for His bride, and we will live with Him in the new Jerusalem. He will give us eternal life!

Look all around you, and realize that God was and is much better than fair. It was we who created this mess— the poverty, the sickness, the death. We gave away our right to sonship, and God has graciously made a way for us to regain it. God is not only fair; He is merciful. He is compassionate. He embodies love. He never quits.

Jesus freely accepted the responsibility to come here and pay the price for us. He was beaten, whipped and tortured; He took all the sin and rebellion of mankind upon Himself. He gave His blood in exchange for our freedom. Then He went to Hell and back, and He rose again the third day! He won the victory!

He did this for us, and I ask you this: Was that fair?

A SERVANT'S HEART

Let's Pray.

Father, in the name of Jesus, please forgive us for ever thinking that You are unfair, or that You had anything to do with the mess our world is in. Forgive us if we have ever blamed You for sickness or disease. We repent because You gave us life and health, and we gave it all away. We accept the responsibility, and we are so thankful that Jesus came, won our lives back, and gave us eternal life. He paid the high price for us, and we thank You with all our hearts. In His holy name, amen.

Double for Trouble

SOMETIMES LIFE SEEMS TO continually throw us curve balls. You may feel as if you're swinging and swinging, hitting nothing but air. Like a baseball player up to bat, you're not sure what kind of pitch will be thrown.

Your stance is right and your training kicks in as the ball comes toward you at record-breaking speed.

You use all your strength to swing.

Whoosh.

"Strike!"

Three times. You're out.

As you walk away in defeat, thoughts tirelessly bombard you. "If only I had hit that ball…" The strike-out plays over and over in your mind.

Just like a discouraged baseball player, our minds can keep us in a place of trouble if we're not careful. We can look at our problems and mistakes and listen to the inner voice that says, "If only I would have done this, or I wouldn't have done that, then life would be better."

That is not how God sees your life. He says, "I'll give you My double for your trouble."

God doesn't see life through the limited scope of your vision, " 'For My thoughts are not your thoughts, nor are your ways My ways,' says the Lord" (Isaiah 55:8, NKJV).

His double for your trouble is fulfilled through the Holy Spirit in you. He is all you need, and He has revealed Himself as your:

Light in Genesis
Freedom in Exodus
Blessing in Deuteronomy
Courage in Joshua
Faithfulness in Job
Refuge in the Psalms
Wisdom in the Proverbs
Deliverer in Daniel
Seed in Matthew
Bread of Life in John
Power in Acts
Bridegroom in Revelation

The Holy Spirit is love, and He resides in you! The Lord knew that this journey would not be easy. He knows the pitcher, whose name is Satan. And He knows that Satan can throw some high-speed balls, so God made sure to give us His double for the trouble of this life. He imparts His own Spirit in us. "Or do you not know that your body is the temple of the Holy Spirit who is in you, whom you have from God, and you are not your own?" (1 Corinthians 6:19, NKJV).

Understand that you are up against an evil force in this world. Satan and his demons know how to bring pain and discouragement, and they seek only to hurt you.

But also remember that God has placed Himself within you. He gave you all that you need and more to conquer Satan. Throughout your journey, God will breathe His strength, endurance, patience, peace and joy into your life.

There isn't an umpire to shout, "Three strikes, you're out!" in His kingdom. The kingdom of God is full of mercy, love and forgiveness. With Him in your life, no matter what, you will win!

Now go, step up to that plate, take your stance, and when you swing, watch what the Lord will do!

A SERVANT'S HEART

Let's Pray.

Father, in the name of Jesus we receive your strength, patience and peace. Amen.

Compromise

T HE WORLD PRESENTS COMPROMISE as if it is a type of delicacy. It is viewed as something fine, like a table of delicious dainties set before us. We can walk by the table with our plate and choose one over the other, or maybe a couple of each.

But what is compromise? Let's take a look at the word's meaning according to *Webster's Dictionary*:

Noun

1. A middle way between two extremes.

Verb

1. Make a compromise; arrive at a compromise; "nobody will get everything he wants; we all must compromise"

This definition accurately depicts how we have been taught to understand compromise. We see it as a must in our lives. It's not a matter of, "Should I compromise?" but, "When will I compromise, and how much?" We have been taught that if we don't compromise, then we won't get everything we want. And so it has become a must.

This is the way most people live their lives. It is the "right" way to live, the only way to get along with everyone, the best way to fit in. Or so we are taught.

All of this occurs because we seek something called "unity." If you aren't willing to compromise, then you don't really want unity. Anything outside the realm of compromise is presented as harsh, unforgiving and absolutely un-accepting.

It's comparable to eating sweets: They look delicious when they are laid out on the table, and they taste so good. Oh, but later, you don't feel so well. All that sugar starts talking to you; "Why did you eat that? You know how bad you feel right now! Never eat that many sweets at one time again!"

In other words, you pay a price. No matter how gorgeous the sweets look or how yummy they taste, you pay a price for your unhealthy choices.

This is a picture of our lives and the decisions we make every day. You can tell yourself that compromising is a necessary part of life and not a choice, that it is a way to get along with everyone for the sake of unity. It may look good at the time. It may even seem like the easier way to go at the moment. And it can bring you peace for a short time.

But later, there is a price to pay for compromising. It will begin to talk to you, saying, "How did you end up in this mess? Why did I agree to do this?" Once you're in too deep, it will convince you that there is no way out.

Well, that, too, is a lie. There is *always* a way out. Jesus came to us for that very reason: to provide a way out. It doesn't matter where you are or what you've done in your life. Ask Him to forgive you and help you, and He surely will.

Listen: Any problem, from debt, to addiction (whether it's an addiction to food, alcohol, drugs, sex or pornography) does *not* shock or appall your God! He is not sitting on His throne, looking down on you, saying, "Jesus, look at the mess they're in. They are too far gone. We can't use them for anything. Let's just toss them in the 'Used and Abused' pile."

No, a thousand times no! He is the Healer, the Forgiver and the Restorer. He is saying, "Jesus, look at them! Finally, they are calling out for help! Let's go to them right now! We can use them to help others who are struggling. I'm so excited to help them and to bless others through them!"

Everything you've compromised in your life, God can use to help others to either not make the same mistake or to overcome the harmful effects of their choices. Through the example of your life, He can show them hope and freedom. Never underestimate the power of true empathy in the kingdom of God.

We need to start living in an extreme way— extremely healed, extremely blessed, extremely free from addictions and control. Yes, living for the Lord Jesus Christ is extreme. Right is right, and wrong is wrong. But it brings life, peace and joy. It is extremely wonderful to be extreme.

Aren't you tired of living in the middle? Do not be like a donkey that stands between two bales of hay, not knowing which one to eat from, and thus starves to death. Don't stand in the middle of life, looking at the kingdom of God as one bale of hay and compromise as the other, trying to figure out which to eat from. You'll starve to death.

A SERVANT'S HEART

Let's Pray.

Holy Spirit, in the name of Jesus, help us to live free from compromise. Show us how to make extreme decisions for You and in You. We know that this type of living will give us peace, joy, strength and wisdom, and it will bring us life and life more abundantly. In Jesus' name, amen.

Empowered

J ESUS CAME FOR ONE reason: to empower you to once again live as a child of God. We once sold our lives and our right to dominion over the Earth. He took the sins of the world upon Himself to give us back what we gave away.

Genesis 3 records that Satan spoke to Eve and deceived her. He convinced her to defy God's only command: "[Y]ou must not eat from the tree of the knowledge of good and evil, for when you eat from it you will certainly die" (Genesis 2:17, NIV).

This may be a bit easier to understand for those who have children. A parent's well-intended command to a child is not a way to rule over them; it is a way to protect them from harm. Parents want the best and the most for their children. They lay down the "do's" and the "don'ts" so that their children can walk in peace and blessing.

When God created Adam and Eve, He gave them complete rule over the Earth and told them to multiply, fill it and have dominion over it (Genesis 1:28). Then He gave them the one and only "don't" so that they could live in perfect harmony, peace and power!

But man didn't listen to the Lord, and instead he did the only thing God had advised against. Consequently, man lost it all. He gave it to Satan who then became the "god of this world" (2 Corinthians 4:4, KJV).

Jesus came and died, and He paid the penalty for the mistake man made in the Garden. Then He gave it all back to us in the form of salvation!

And so, we have been given the gift of **empowerment**! Now we must learn how to use it again, for with every gift, one needs training.

We are no longer servants of God but His sons and daughters; "that is what we are!" (1 John 3:1, NIV).

We are no longer subject to addiction, but empowered to rule over our fleshly desires. "[T]he Lord will make you the head and not the tail; you shall be above only, and not be beneath" (Deuteronomy 28:13, NKJV).

You might say to yourself, "Not the way I'm living! That's not happening here!" That is *only* true because you have not been trained to walk in your God-given empowerment. He has placed within you the power to say "No," and you have His permission to do so.

Your voice is your trainer, and it is free. Start today. Speak the truth into whatever area of your life needs freedom or success.

Look in the mirror, grab yourself by the collar and say, "I'm in charge here, and Flesh, you will not overeat today! Do you hear me? I'm telling you what you're going to do now! You will not make decisions for me!"

Oh yes, you have to train your body to do what you say. Your flesh— that is, your body and its carnal desires— is like a child. You have to tell it to get up out of that warm bed in the morning and go to work. You have to tell it to exercise and shower. You have to tell it what to watch on TV and what not to watch. You have to tell it what to eat and when to stop eating. In the store, you have to tell it, "You're not getting that today!" just as if you're talking to a child.

We teach children as they grow so that they will one day be empowered with wisdom to be good stewards of God's freedom and blessings. You might think it impossible to successfully live with freedom and blessings in every area of your life. But why else would Jesus have said that "with God all things are possible" (Matthew 19:26, NKJV)?

This truth is for you today! Start training your body what to do. Teach it, talk to it. It must do what you say; after all, it is subject to your will.

A SERVANT'S HEART

Let's Pray.

Father, in the name of Jesus, help us to teach, train and talk to our bodies and our fleshly desires. We desire to be free and blessed in every area of our lives. We know that Jesus came to empower us to live abundant, successful lives, and He died so that we could regain control over our sinful natures. We will live according to this purpose in Your name, Jesus, for You are the Key that always unlocks this door. We thank You for everything You have done and will do. In Jesus' name, amen.

The Perfect Day

DO YOU REMEMBER SUMMER VACATIONS as a kid? The first thing on your mind was: "Let's wake up and start having fun! Who am I going to play with today?"

Your biggest concern was what kind of fun you were going to have, but one thing was certain: Fun was what you were going to make happen! You would bounce out of bed, eat some cereal, watch some cartoons, and then start making phone calls, or maybe just dive into some games with your brothers and sisters.

Regardless of what it was, summer days were centered on fun. They were spent giggling, swimming, roller-skating and playing hide-and-seek.

And as the curtain of night slowly draped over the sky, you would hop into bed and drift off to sleep with a little sunburn on your face, only to repeat the process the next day.

What happened to that little person? I can hear you answer, "I grew up."

When you wake up in the morning now, what is your first thought? How many times a day do you laugh? Do you ever make plans to just go out and have some fun?

You have to take control of your days, or they will control you. You took control when you were little, thought you probably didn't realize it. You scheduled fun, and made plans accordingly! You called other kids, or you played with your siblings. You made it happen, and plenty of fun was had.

We have to do the same in our adult lives. Work and all the responsibilities of life will swallow you up or pin you down until fun is nowhere to be found. Even if you enjoy your work or your responsibilities, they don't qualify as intentional fun for fun's sake. You rarely let your hair down anymore, or your laughter out.

But, when you allow yourself to tap into fun, joy will well up from deep inside you. The Word of God says, "A merry heart does good, like medicine" (Proverbs 17:22, NKJV).

Laughter, joy and fun are essential to healthy lives. It really isn't an option, but a required need. As food and water are to your body, so is laughter to your soul.

I'm not talking about scheduling fun for your kids or someone else. I'm talking about scheduling fun for *yourself*. God created joy to be a part of our daily lives, and it should not be neglected. Proverbs 17:22 goes on to say that your bones will dry up without it.

It may take some time to get used to scheduling fun into your life. It will also take some thought: "What can I do to have fun?" It may have been a while since you thought about it.

But watch how your spirit changes when you make time for pure fun. You will feel and seem healthier from the inside out. You will laugh, and life will bubble up in your heart. You will enjoy the days in a new way.

Then, when you lie down in bed and night's curtain drapes over the sky, you will dream of the joys of tomorrow. And you're all grown up!

A Servant's Heart

Let's Pray.

Holy Spirit, in the name of Jesus, we ask You to remind us daily to schedule fun for ourselves. Reveal Yourself as the God of joy, peace and laughter who created us to live joyfully. You created laughter to heal our bodies like medicine; show us how fun can bring life and health into our dry bones. Holy Spirit, help us to bring joy into our own lives and the lives of the people around us. We need to remember not to take life so seriously; there is always room for fun. In Jesus' name, amen.

The Line in the Sand

THERE WAS A TIME when Jesus stood up for someone— someone who was surely condemned to death.

Jesus came to set us free, but in order to do so He had to keep all the laws of the Old Testament. He said, "Do not think that I have come to abolish the Law or the Prophets; I have not come to abolish them but to fulfill them" (Matthew 5:17, NIV).

Jesus lived a sinless life, but He was sentenced to death for our crimes. Only through His innocent blood could God save us and establish His new order in which "[m]ercy triumphs over judgment" (James 2:13, NKJV).

In one account, a teacher of the law asked Jesus which commandment was the greatest;

> Jesus answered him, "**The first of all** the commandments is, Hear, O Israel; The Lord our God is one Lord:
>
> And thou shalt love the Lord thy God with all thy heart, and with all thy soul, and with all thy mind, and with all thy strength: this is the first commandment.
>
> And the second is like, namely this, Thou shalt love thy neighbour as thyself. There is none other commandment greater than these" (Mark 12:29-30, KJV, emphasis mine).

Essentially, Jesus changed the subject from God's judgment to His immense love.

But the religious leaders knew that in order for Jesus to be the true Messiah, He would have to be perfect, and that would require keeping all the laws. So one day, the scribes and Pharisees brought a woman to Jesus, and "they said to Him, 'Teacher, this woman was caught in adultery, in the very act. **Now Moses, in the law, commanded us** that such should be stoned. But what do You say?' " (John 8:4-5, NKJV, emphasis mine).

Having heard Jesus' message of love and compassion, they wanted to see how He would handle this difficult situation. "They were using this question as a trap, in order to have a basis for accusing him" (John 8:6, NIV).

Moses was a man of God and a strong leader. In the Pharisees' religious minds, God would never pardon such a blatant sin as adultery.

So, which law would Jesus follow? Would He disobey the Law of Moses and proclaim a new law, or would He obey Mosaic Law and prove Himself a hypocrite?

The Bible says that Jesus stooped down and began writing in the sand with His finger as though He hadn't even heard them.

They continued to badger Him about the issue until He got up and said, "He who is **without sin among** you, let him throw a stone at her first" (John 8:7, NKJV, emphasis mine).

Then Jesus bent down to the ground again and continued writing in the sand.

The Pharisees and scribes were so convicted of their own sin that they dropped their rocks and left, leaving Jesus alone with the adulteress.

He stood up, looked into her shame-filled eyes and said,

> "Woman, where are those accusers of yours? Has no one condemned you?"
>
> She said, "No one, Lord."

And Jesus said to her, "Neither do I condemn you; go and sin no more" (John 4:10-11, NKJV).

So, Jesus out-foxed the foxes once again. He knew the Pharisees intended to hinder the very purpose for which God had sent Him. This was neither about the woman nor her sin; they used her to set Jesus up for failure. And even worse, they were willing to kill a woman just to prove Him wrong.

Once, as I was wrapping up a box up to send in the mail, the packing tape kept getting lost in itself. As soon as I cut off a piece of tape and let go, the new end would disappear somewhere on the roll. I kept having to tilt the roll of tape sideways to try to distinguish the end. When that didn't work, I would run my fingernail across the roll until I felt the ridge. I did this several times, and when I was almost done, the Holy Spirit spoke to me.

"What is it you're looking for?" He asked.

"I'm looking for the beginning of the tape," I told Him.

"Yes, the line is the beginning," He told me.

A few minutes later, He reminded me of the story of Jesus and the adulteress. I pictured Jesus stooped down, writing in the sand, and in it He drew a line.

The Holy Spirit showed me that the first time Jesus bent down to draw in the sand, He drew a line for the scribes and Pharisees. This line represented their law, the Law of Moses, which could only be fulfilled by stoning the woman for her sin.

The second time He bent down to draw in the sand, Jesus drew a new line to represent the New Covenant in which "love covers over a multitude of sins" (1 Peter 4:8, NKJV).

In so doing, Jesus convicted even the so-called "holiest" men of their sin. Suddenly, the Pharisees realized that not even they could live up to the standards of the Law. They were forced to drop their stones and walk away from their own judgment.

They would rather have seen a woman die than embrace a King who would set her free. They chose the line of judgment over grace, and they were better than everyone else in their society— smarter, richer and more pious. But when they challenged Jesus, He won! He set us free from judgment and portrayed such a sweet picture of the goodness of our God.

So I ask you this question: Which line are you on? Are you judging other people, or do you seek to set them free?

A SERVANT'S HEART

Let's Pray.

Father, in the name of Jesus, we ask You to give us a nudge when we are gossiping about others, whether they have sinned or not. Lord, help us to walk in love for all people. Teach us not to be critical of anyone, but to accept everyone. We recognize that it is not our place to judge them, for You are the one true Judge. We want them to be free and forgiven, just as you forgave us and set us free. In Jesus' name, amen.

Focus on the Hope Ahead

I F YOU ARE LIVING for the Lord Jesus, then you are the prophet of your own life. This is how God has created us. He enables you to navigate your own footsteps and gladly walks with you wherever your footsteps take you.

A friend of mine recently trained for a bike race. His trainer told him, "When you hit a sharp corner, don't look at the curve; look ahead." During the race, the bikers that looked at the turns experienced disastrous results. They either froze and went straight, or they turned too hard, dumping their bikes. But the bikers who looked to the road ahead took to the curves as smoothly as butter.

This is how we should go through life. The Holy Spirit is our Trainer, and He teaches us how to approach the curves in this race of life. The Bible says, "let us run with patience the race that is set before us" (Hebrews 12:1, KJV).

God doesn't want us to focus on the challenges that block our paths; He wants us to look up and meditate on His Word. When you fix your eyes on His Word, it will provide light on your path (Psalm 119:105).

If you focus all your attention on the challenges you face, then you will only hear the reasons why you will never attain the desires of your heart. You will begin to see only the negative because what you listen to will inevitably settle in your heart. Negativity will rob you of your goals and dreams.

This is called "fear," and it is a thief! It comes only to steal, kill and destroy the destiny that God instilled in your heart (see John 10:10).

Look closely at the word "fear." If you remove the 'f', what does it spell? "Ear!" The reasons why you can't or won't succeed are fears that have come through your ears. Negativity might say that you're too old, you don't have enough money, it's too late, or you're not good enough. When you listen to these kinds of thoughts, fear accomplishes its purpose—to abort the mission of your destiny in Christ.

All you have to do is turn on the TV or radio, or listen someone at work or even a family member. When people constantly speak negatively, they can easily plant doubt, discouragement and fear in your spirit. This could end up **aborting your dream** before it is born.

God's Word is contrary to this world's report:

"God is not a man that should lie" (Hebrews 23:19, NKJV).

"My word... shall not return to Me void" (Isaiah 55:11, NKJV).

"[W]ith God all things are possible" (Mark 10:27, NKJV).

"He shall give you the desires of your heart" (Psalm 37:4, NKJV).

"The Lord will make you the head and not the tail" (Deuteronomy 28:13, NKJV).

"I can do all things through Christ who strengthens me" (Philippians 4:13, NKJV).

"[W]hoever... does not doubt in his heart, but believes that those things he says will be done, he will have whatever he says" (Mark 11:23, NKJV).

"Blessed is the one... whose delight is in the law of the Lord, And who meditates on his law day and night" (Psalm 1:1-2, NIV).

"Be strong and of good courage" (Joshua 1:6, NKJV).

"No weapon formed against you shall prosper" (Isaiah 54:17, NKJV).

As much as possible, stop listening to negativity, and double up on the positive sources you listen to. Draw in God's wisdom, and He will fulfill the desires of your heart.

Be the prophet of your own life, follow His Word, and watch where your footsteps take you!

A SERVANT'S HEART

Let's Pray.

Holy Spirit, in the name of Jesus, we ask You to remind us to hold up our shields of faith whenever a negative report comes against us. Teach us to skillfully draw the sword of the Spirit, which is the Word of God. We will stand against all bad reports, for You are our Glory and Lifter of our heads. In Jesus' name, amen.

Snowflakes

Have you ever felt like you don't have enough faith in God, Jesus Christ or the Holy Spirit? What is faith anyway? Take a look at the definition from *Webster's Dictionary Online*:

1. belief and trust in and loyalty to God

2. firm belief in something for which there is no proof (emphasis mine)

3. complete trust

You may think, "How can I believe in something 'for which there is no proof'?" In this entry, I hope to show you.

When you go to bed at night, do you question whether or not you will wake up in the morning? Probably not. Most of us give a goodnight kiss, get things ready for the morning and crawl into bed with full confidence that we will be getting out of bed in the morning. But is there proof? Every morning, you wake up by faith.

Likewise, when you get into your car each day, do you question whether or not you will reach your destination? Most of us drive with full confidence that we will make it. But do we have proof?

How can any of us live with such confidence when we have no idea what each day will bring? This kind of assurance in everyday life did not drop out of the sky and land in your lap. It is a learned behavior.

As we grow up, we watch the people around us and learn from their behavior patterns. We are taught that cars, airplanes, trains and boats do what people want them to do. We also **learn** how to have confidence.

Faith in Jesus Christ is the same. We hear about Him, His love and salvation. And then we **learn** about Him. We go to schools, classes and churches where we learn about how the kingdom of God operates. It is a system, just like the mechanics of a car, our government or the army.

Faith in our Lord Jesus does not drop out of the sky and land on a few of us, missing the rest of humanity. No! Faith in the Lord and the way He operates is a **learned behavior.**

Just like anything, the more you focus on God, the more you learn about Him. He is a Person, as well as a Spirit, with a real, vibrant personality.

The Word says that the Holy Spirit "will teach you all things, and bring to your remembrance **all** things that [Jesus] said" (John 14:26, NKJV, emphasis mine). But you have to put time into your relationship with God in order to know Him well, just as you would with your spouse or a close friend.

God is not holding back anything from you; He is patiently waiting for you to ask. Ask Him to teach you, to show you, to prove things to you. I promise you, when we ask with a sincere heart, He **always** responds. But you must always remain teachable before your God, for He will never (and simply cannot) prove anything to you when you ask with arrogance in your heart. He will faithfully respond when you ask in humble honesty.

The Lord knows who is genuine and who is not. Remember, He created you! He knows everything about you, down to the numbers of the hairs on your head (Matthew 10:30).

You may say, "Prove it!"

Okay, I have one question for you. You have probably heard that there are no two identical snowflakes, that they all have a unique design. We all have heard this, and most of us simply accept it as truth. I say, prove it. If you can believe that about snowflakes with no element of proof, then you most assuredly can have faith in the Lord.

Don't ever think that you don't have enough faith; you just need to learn more about your God. He is real, and when you meet Him, you'll know! And then, you won't need proof.

A Servant's Heart

Let's Pray.

Father, in the name of Jesus, we ask You to teach us about Your Son and the ways of Your kingdom. We want to grow in faith by seeking You. We understand that faith isn't something that falls from the sky; it comes as we learn more about You through experience. Teach us, give us revelations, and take us to the next level in our relationships with You. We thank You. In Jesus' name, amen.

Posture

L OOKING AT A PERSON's posture can tell you a lot about them. When someone walks into a room with their back straight, their shoulders pulled back and their head held high, you presume that they are confident. Each step they take makes a statement with a little attitude: "I'm a winner. I'm a go-getter."

It's attractive— not necessarily in the physical sense, but their confidence draws people to them.

Why? Because they seem so full of life! If you take a moment to look at people, you won't see much of that out there. So, when you do see it, it's breathtaking.

Generally, people walk around as if they are carrying their house on their shoulders and their car on their back. They look tired and worn out.

This is true because physical posture usually mirrors spiritual posture. Your spiritual body forms the frame for your physical body just like the wood that makes up the frame of a house. Builders know that a good foundation and a solid frame are the keys to a strong house. A house's frame determines how it will hold up over time and under stress.

Likewise, the condition of your spiritual health determines how well you will fair in the storms of life and the journey of aging. Time will inevitably reveal how strong your spirit is. Some people who aren't even fifty years old look worn-out, while others in their seventies beam with life. Age has little to do with how strong your posture is; this has to do with the inner man.

The more you strengthen your spirit through a relationship with the Holy Spirit, the more you strengthen your frame. We must make love, joy and forgiveness the foundation of our frames.

If you do this, I guarantee that your spiritual posture will be strong, healthy and alive. Your physical body will mirror that confidence, and you will stand up straight and strong.

Concentrate on developing a strong spiritual posture from this point forward, just as you would follow a physical exercise plan. Make time to talk with the Holy Spirit, pray, and read and listen to positive messages. If you do this at least once a day, you will literally begin to stand a little taller, walk a little faster, and you may even feel as if you have lost some dead weight.

And, actually, you have. Just turn around, and you'll see the car and the house that you once carried on your back now laying on the ground. Don't go back and pick them up; just keep on walking.

A SERVANT'S HEART

Let's Pray.

Father, in the name of Jesus, we ask the Holy Spirit to be our Coach in losing the weight of this world. Help us to make time and take the time to seek You in prayer and to focus on the fact that we can do all things through Christ who strengthens us daily (Philippians 4:13). Strengthen our spiritual beings so that we will know in increasing depth how much more important You are than anything else in life. When our spiritual bodies are strong, we will be the people You have called us to be. Help us, Lord, to be whom we need to be for our friends, our families and our jobs. In Jesus' name, amen.

Rewind

HIS MERCIES ARE NEW every morning (Lamentations 3:23). Every day is a **new** day. Isn't that exciting?

Recall your days in school as a child, when the teacher would write on the chalkboard all day long. At the end of the day, it was crammed with information. And just before the end of the school day, she would choose someone to erase the board. It was washed completely clean, ready for a new day.

This is a clear picture of our lives. When you go to bed at night, no matter what has taken place that day, the board is washed clean. When you wake up each morning, the Word of God says, "Through the Lord's mercies we are not consumed, Because His compassions fail not. They are new every morning" (Lamentations 3:22-23, NKJV).

The Word also says that "The Lord... daily loads us with benefits" (Psalm 68:19, NKJV). If you have a job, or if you have insurance, then you understand what "benefits" are; they are "the gain of something, a positive" (*Webster's Dictionary*).

Not only are God's mercies new every morning, but every day, He gives you a positive start and blesses every area of your life— and not just a little bit! The Word says He "**loads**" us with His benefits!

This applies to every area of our lives— financial, social, emotional, physical and spiritual. All this, every day, and it's free! What a God we serve. No employer can match this deal. Just think, no matter what mistakes we make today, or have ever made, or will ever make, God's abundant blessings await us every morning.

God's mercies are "**new**" every morning. Think about how much we value a new beginning, a chance at a fresh start. Once a year, we make it a point to celebrate this occasion on a night we call "New Year's Eve." We make great plans for this day. We get all dressed up, brave bad weather, celebrate at big dinners and parties with our closest friends and families.

Why? Because we eagerly welcome a **new** beginning. One day a year, we give ourselves permission to rewind the recorder that has been documenting all of our bad habits and wrong decisions over the past 365 days. And on this one evening, we get to erase all of it, start over and call it a "New Year."

This is our own, once-a-year benefit, but God gives us permission to have this celebration every single day. He made a way for us so that we don't have to wait all year to wipe our boards clean. He wants us to wake up every morning with joy, peace and excitement.

Today is a new day. You are forgiven, healed and blessed— no matter what. God's Word says that "joy comes in the morning" (Psalm 30:5, NKJV). All you have to do is give yourself permission to accept this gift.

Get up today, tomorrow, and the next; get dressed, go out and find someone to celebrate with!

A SERVANT'S HEART

Let's Pray.

Father, in the name of Jesus, please teach us to wake up daily with the knowledge that Your mercies are new every morning, and they never run out. Show us how You "load" Your benefits upon our lives daily. Help us to give ourselves permission to celebrate today as a new day. We thank You for erasing our past mistakes and enabling us walk in new joy. In Jesus' name, amen.

To Dance, or Not to Dance

SERVING THE LORD IS not always the popular way to live. In the world, right sometimes seems wrong, while wrong is deemed right.

If you dare to stand up for basic moral values, the world might just condemn you as a judgmental extremist who lacks any form of compassion. But if you instead embrace the sin set before you, it holds no relief for you either. The world will only place something else before you, demanding that you compromise in that area as well.

Despite all that you give, someone will always determine that it's not enough. If you live for others, you will end up confused, discouraged and worn out.

Trying to please everyone is impossible. No matter what you do or say, it will never be enough. Many godly men, including Jesus, confronted the same harsh reality, so rest assured that you're in good company.

John the Baptist was sent by God to prepare the way for the Messiah— the One who would come to save the world from its sin. John was not exactly what one would call, "well kept," but he was a man who knew his mission. He pursued his God-given purpose and fulfilled it, whether public opinion favored him or not. He would have much preferred to be rejected by men than to step away from his calling from the Lord. So he stayed in the wilderness, preaching and waiting for the day that Jesus would come.

Many who heard John embraced his message, but the religious leaders of his day stood back with their arms crossed and their minds made up. They did not condone anything he said or did, and they pressed him to be like them. When John refused, they rejected him and said to themselves, "He is not the man to follow; he is not sent from God."

But Jesus came, just as John the Baptist prophesied. He lived, died and shed His blood for the sins of the world. He, too, preferred to stand alone and die for God's purpose than to compromise His destiny.

Many people who heard Jesus embraced His message, but the religious leaders again stood off to the side with their arms folded and their minds made up, saying, "He doesn't look like someone God would send because He doesn't embrace our teachings or our ways." Because Jesus did not affirm their prideful hearts, they rejected Him.

Jesus responded to them and said,

> For John the Baptist came neither eating bread nor drinking wine, and you say, "He has a demon." The Son of Man has come eating and drinking, and you say, "Look, a glutton and a winebibber, a friend of tax collectors and sinners!" But wisdom is justified by all her children (Luke 7:33-35, NKJV).

Basically, the Pharisees told John to dance, and then they told Jesus not to dance. They were set in their cynical ways.

So don't judge your calling by who accepts you; just be sure that you are humbly walking out God's purpose for your life. God will embrace you as you embrace Him.

As His Word says, "If God is for us, who can be against us?" (Romans 8:31, NKJV). **Be strong and courageous.** Live with wisdom and determination. Walk in love, and be whom the Lord leads you to be!

A SERVANT'S HEART

Let's Pray.

Holy Spirit, in the name of Jesus, we ask You to fill us with boldness, confidence and determination to be whom You have called us to be. We don't look for acceptance from people, but we long for Your love and Your presence. In Jesus' name, amen.

I strongly encourage you to read the Gospel of Luke in its entirety. It holds such wisdom and encouragement from the life of Christ.

The Blame Game

As wonderful as life can be, it is not without disappointments. The Bible says, "To every thing there is a season, and a time to every purpose under the heaven" (Ecclesiastes 3:1, KJV).

Yes, there is a time for everything, every milestone, every emotion. And this includes pain.

Pain is an emotion, and it has a voice. Sometimes it says, "I'm hurting inside. Please, someone, stop this pain; I can't take it anymore." It's looking for a way out, like steam trying to escape from a pressure cooker. It searches for room to expand but finds none.

Because pain is so uncomfortable, we will do anything to get rid of it. This is where we need to be careful. Sometimes we look for a scapegoat—someone to blame so that we can rid ourselves of pressure. We allow blinders to cover our eyes, and we point a finger at others, saying, "If only *you* would have done this, or if *you* wouldn't have said that, then I wouldn't be hurting this much."

In reality, the best thing we can do is turn to God in the midst of our pain and pray, "Lord Jesus, my heart is hurting right now. I'm asking You to help me not to blame anyone else for my pain. Show me how to forgive those who have hurt me, just as You have forgiven me. I turn my hurt over to You; help me to overcome this problem by Your strength."

The Lord is the *only* one who can handle the weight of all our problems, and He has promised to turn it all around for your good, if you will let

Him (Romans 8:28). But, if you insist on blaming someone else, then God cannot move on your behalf.

You are right to want to be rid of pain. It must leave your heart, for you were not created to endure this emotion for long period of time. That's why it brings so much pressure. Thankfully, God made a way for you to release that pressure in a healthy way.

No matter who did or said what, you can always go to the Lord and give it all to Him. And He will set you free from it all. Isn't that what we're all looking for? Freedom!

Release yourself today; forgive those who have hurt you. And I promise you, joy will enter your heart. Choose today to live in joy! It's your choice.

A Servant's Heart

Let's Pray.

Father, in the name of Jesus, please take our away our pain and past hurts. We forgive everyone in our lives who has hurt us. We don't want to blame them, Father. You forgave all of our sins, and we choose to forgive others. We understand that we might still feel the same way for a time, but we know that when we give this problem to You, in time, the pain will leave, and joy will come. Thank You for giving us the strength to overcome this. In Jesus' name, amen.

Be blessed in His love.

Covenant

GOD CREATED MALE AND female, and as the Word says, they became one flesh (Genesis 2:24).

When a man meets the woman of his dreams, he falls in love with her and finds himself consumed with thoughts of her day and night. He desires to be with her all the time, to watch her eyes sparkle and her soft hair fall on her shoulders. He adores her sweet perfume and the soft touch of her hand. He dreams of taking his pure bride home to be with him after she says, "I do."

His heart is determined to protect her, hold her and love her all the days of his life. He watches over his household because he knows that she is good and worth protecting. He would never let anyone steal her heart from him.

Her words are governed by kindness, and he knows that he can trust her heart. He loves his bride, and forever a bride she will be in his eyes.

These two have become one flesh.

Blood was shed when she gave all of herself to him. The ring on her finger speaks without words, "I belong to you, my husband." She took his name with honor. She guards her heart and protects her merchandise. She skillfully manages their household, and there is no idleness in her.

One day, Jesus will return for His bride, the church (see Revelation 21). Just as a man waits for his bride, Jesus is earnestly waiting for you. He has built chambers for you to dwell in (John 14:2). He looks forward to the day when He will take you away forever into His kingdom. He dreams of your eyes and your hair:

Behold, you are fair, my love!

Behold, you are fair!

You have dove's eyes behind your veil.

Your hair is like a flock of goats,

Going down from Mount Gilead...

You are all fair, my love,

And there is no spot in you...

You have ravished my heart,

My sister, my spouse;

You have ravished my heart

With one look of your eyes (Song of Solomon 4:1, 7, 9, NKJV).

Jesus is in love with His church. He will forever protect you from the enemy that tries to deceive you. He gave His life for you, and He will not rest until He is with you. He counts the days until He can come for you.

And the two shall become one.

God is also coming back to restore the Earth: "The earth is the Lord's, and the fullness thereof" (Psalm 24:1, KJV). "[T]he earth shall cast out the dead" (Isaiah 26:19, KJV).

You are the one whom Jesus loves, and He thinks about you always. He adores your laugh and delights in the twinkle of your eyes. He longs to protect you, love you and embrace you. And you have taken on His name with honor. You gave up everything for Him, and He for you. Him only will you serve.

He knows that the enemy is watching for opportunities to steal your heart from Him, but He watches over you with a husband's heart. "For I am jealous over you with godly jealousy: for I have espoused you to one husband, that I may present you as a chaste virgin to Christ" (2 Corinthians 11:2, KJV).

God gave His only Son for you; He fought for you and is still fighting. He waits with a longing heart. "Our God shall come, and shall not keep silence: a fire shall devour before him, and it shall be very tempestuous round about him" (Psalm 50:3, KJV).

He has made a covenant with you:

> But my faithfulness and my mercy shall be with him: and in my name shall his horn be exalted. I will set his hand also in the sea, and his right hand in the rivers. He shall cry unto me, Thou art my father, my God, and the rock of my salvation. Also I will make him my firstborn, higher than the kings of the earth. My mercy will I keep for him for evermore, and my **covenant** shall stand fast with him. His seed also will I make to endure for ever, and his throne as the days of heaven (Psalm 89:24-29, KJV, emphasis mine).

And on the great day of His return, trumpets shall blow, angels shall sing, and **Heaven and Earth shall become one!** Let those that have ears hear the Word of the Lord (Revelation 2:17).

A SERVANT'S HEART

Let's Pray.

Father, in the name of Jesus, reveal Your heart to us. In Jesus' name, amen.

Be blessed in His love.

Silence

Have you ever experienced an extended period of loneliness in your life?

Maybe it was in college before you were married, and although you would go to big parties, you felt like the only voice you could hear was the one in your head, saying, "Why is this room so quiet and empty?"

Or maybe you were in church, and everyone around you was lifting their hands high with smiles on their faces as if they could see something glorious beyond the ceiling. You looked up and saw only the dust hanging from the lights.

Whatever the instance, perhaps at some point you've felt like screaming, "When will this silence SHUT UP? How can I make this silence be quiet?"

You're not the only one who has ever felt this way; Jesus encountered the same struggle. When He was brought before Pilate just before His crucifixion, "Pilate unto him, Hearest thou not how many things they witness against thee? And he answered him to never a word; insomuch that the governor marveled greatly" (Matthew 27:13-14, KJV). Jesus answered with silence because sometimes, silence resonates more profoundly than words.

In times when you feel like no matter what you do, a deep sense of silence haunts your heart, don't believe the lie that you are alone. Don't be afraid of the silence, and don't clutter your life with activities and people just to drown it out.

A quiet season can actually be a time of separation from the world. It is a time to embrace the stillness and let silence teach you. As the Holy Spirit draws you out of one season of your life, He will allow a time of transition to take you to the next level of your life with Him.

Realize that times of silence are rich treasures that can teach us the value of patience and faith. Listen, pray, and ask the Lord, "What are You doing right now, and where are we going?" You are not alone; He is breathing new life into your bones. Allow Him to lead you, one soft step at a time.

When the silence breaks, you will be more mature, and a new fire will glow within you— the fire of the Holy Spirit. What God can (and surely will) do is powerful and precious.

The next time you can't get seem to quiet the silence, quiet your thoughts and watch what the Lord will do with your patience and trust. He will take you to new levels and give you a greater anointing. When you come out, your life will be a joyous testimony of His faithfulness.

A Servant's Heart

Let's Pray.

Holy Spirit, in the name of Jesus, we ask You to remind us that times of silence are precious opportunities in which You draw us away from the noise of this world. Help us to see them as sweet times to commune with You and grow in Your love. Teach us to embrace the quiet and to encounter You amidst the silence. Strengthen us through these moments, and teach us not to be afraid. We give our whole hearts to You in Jesus' name. Amen.

The Mind

THE MIND AND THE brain are not the same. Your brain is like a computer. It collects and stores unlimited amounts of information. It is also the power center for your body. It controls speech and coordination, and is sort of the hard drive for your life. Whatever information you download into your memory, your brain will use to operate your life.

Have you ever heard someone say, "That's it. I've reached my limit. I can't learn any more. I'm going to have to stop now. My brain is full."?

Our brains don't have a limited capacity. From the time you are born until the day you die, your brain will never be full. From that fact alone, one must perceive that there is a God. What a Creator He is! He is the epitome of imagination.

Just as the brain is the body's computer and the ruler over our physical senses, the mind is also a type of control center. Our minds govern our spiritual beings. Like the brain, there is no limit to the amount of information the mind can take in.

However, the mind is much more powerful than the brain. United with God, it has the ability to overrule the brain. The mind was created to be the ruler.

Your mind controls your outlook on life. Its perspective is the difference between living a victorious and a defeated lifestyle. It controls your perception of every matter and determines whether you will be a fighter or a quitter.

Your mind is you! It reaches out to touch your dreams while you sleep.

Satan knows exactly how important the human mind is. Remember, he was there when you were created. If you were him, and you were in a fight with God, what would you do? If you wanted to destroy man, would you not attack his central life-force? There lies Satan's plan for revenge against God. He strategically attacks our minds. The Word of God says that "the god of this world [Satan] hath blinded the minds of them which believeth not" (2 Corinthians 4:4, KJV).

Satan has always waged spiritual warfare against the minds of God's people, and as it continues to prove extremely effective, he will continue to do it. He uses the same tactics over and over, and we all know that practice makes you perfect. By now, his tactics must be well refined.

However, God's Word says, "Yet in all these things we are more than conquerors through Him who loved us" (Romans 8:37, NKJV).

Use your mind to read, listen to and see the things of God, and let Him transform you "by the renewing of your mind" (Romans 12:2, NKJV). Those who patiently spend time in His presence will mature to their full potential. You have the capacity to have the mind of Christ (1 Corinthians 2:16). It is foolish to let this profound gift sit idle within us.

Why would we spend all of our time accumulating knowledge in our brains but neglect our minds, which govern our bodies? This is comparable to hanging the moon in the place of the sun and commanding it to give us heat and light. It could not do it. We spend years training our brains, and then hope to walk on water, heal the sick and move mountains.

The brain cannot be the mind. The mind is the source of your life; it is your being, your spirit. It decides your dreams and says, "I can," when everyone else tells you that you can't.

God's Word says, "Put on the full armor of God, so that you can take your stand against the devil's schemes... Take the helmet of salvation and the sword of the Spirit... And pray in the Spirit on all occasions with all kinds of prayers and requests. With this in mind, be alert" (Ephesians 6:11, 17-18, NIV).

Put your helmet on to protect your mind from the god of this world. You will rule over every area of your life. Remember, you can do all things through Christ because He gives you strength (Philippians 4:13).

A Servant's Heart

Let's Pray.

Father, in the name of Jesus, we ask You to teach us how to reach our full potential. We desire to spend time with You and to be filled with Your anointing. We want to become sources of Your great power in this world so that its people can experience Your glory in real, tangible and personal ways. They will only see Your glory through us. In Jesus' name, amen.

Be blessed in His love.

Times of War and Peace

PEACE IN YOUR HOME and in your nation is a sweet thing, like a fragrant perfume drifting effortlessly through the air. And with peace comes freedom.

We have the freedom to be all that the Lord has called us to be. Many have fought to their deaths for the freedom, of our children and our nation. We will give our own lives so that the spirit of freedom can reign.

And that is the Lord's Spirit— the Spirit of Freedom. The Apostle Paul wrote, "Now the Lord is the Spirit, and where the Spirit of the Lord is, there is freedom" (2 Corinthians 3:17, NIV). The Spirit of Freedom has many names:

"I AM THAT I AM" (Exodus 3:14, KJV),

"I am Alpha and Omega" (Revelation 1:8, KJV),

He is alive and well. He, too, will fight until the end to restore peace to the kingdom of Heaven. God sent His only Son to the world as His best solider to fight for your freedom. And He won! His victory was sealed in the blood of Jesus. But we are still in battle against His arch enemy.

Satan holds the lease to this world for the remainder of its time. But, when the lease is up, there will be freedom from Lucifer's nest for the soldiers of the Lord's army. But during this short (but seemingly long) interim, Satan still battles with God. He is trying to take out as many of God's people as he can, before we can tell everyone that there is a place of eternal peace and freedom, and win more souls for the Lord's kingdom.

But the Lord has given us His Holy Spirit to use as a compass and His written Word to use as a map so that we will be safe from Satan's traps until He returns. He also gave us specific instructions for battle through one of His commanding generals, the Apostle Paul:

> Put on the whole armour of God, that ye may be able to stand against the wiles of the devil.
>
> For we wrestle not against flesh and blood, but against principalities, against powers, against the rulers of the darkness of this world, against spiritual wickedness in high places.
>
> Wherefore take unto you the whole armour of God, that ye may be able to stand in the evil day, and having done all, to stand.
>
> Stand therefore, having your loins girt about with truth, and having on the breastplate of righteousness;
>
> And your feet shod with the preparation of the gospel of peace;
>
> Above all, taking the shield of faith, wherewith ye shall be able to quench all the fiery darts of the wicked.
>
> And take the helmet of salvation, and the sword of the Spirit, which is the word of God:
>
> Praying always with all prayer and supplication in the Spirit, and watching thereunto with all perseverance and supplication for all saints (Ephesians 6:11-18, KJV).

This is a directive from our Commander, not a suggestion. We are in a battle, and we will be in it until the Lord Jesus Christ comes back for His church. We will fight until the end, when once again we will enjoy God's sweet peace and freedom like fragrance after the rain, for all eternity. And eternity is a long, long time to be free.

A Servant's Heart

Let's Pray.

Father, You gave us instructions to take this world by force in the power of the name of Jesus. We ask the Holy Spirit to put His fire within us, so we can take back this land for You while we wait for Your return. We want to tell everyone that You love them and You're not angry with them. We want to give them Your salvation in Jesus' name. Amen.

A Heart of Thorns

W HEN SOMEONE DOES SOMETHING selfless, we often say, "They have a heart of gold." We admire them for being strong enough to take care of others, while maintaining a tender heart. They see the needs of friends, family and strangers and choose to be the vessel that pours blessing into their lives. It doesn't matter how much money they have in the bank; they give from what they have. They pour out their time and energy to meet the needs of others, and the more they give, the bigger their heart gets. There is pep in their step, and their smile could melt snow. Their life is like a bowl of fruit, healthy and full of color.

In the Parable of the Sower, Jesus taught us how to open up our hearts and to rely on them instead of the world's logic (Mark 4:3-20). Essentially, He was saying to His disciples, "When you hear from the Lord, **what do you do with the information?**"

God continually gives us information regarding every situation, including whatever you are going through right now. But if your heart is so full of problems that you're unable or unwilling to listen, then His counsel will not help you. He said, "And some [information] fell among thorns, and the thorns grew up, and choked it, and it yielded no fruit" (Mark 4:7, KJV).

Jesus later explained this parable: "And these are they which are sown among thorns; such as **hear the word [His counsel]**, And the cares of this world, and the deceitfulness of riches, and the lusts of other things entering in, choke the word, and it becometh unfruitful" (Mark 4:18-19, KJV).

So, if your heart is consumed with the problems of this world, then the cares of this world can surround the God's truth and destroy it. Worldly logic often counters the Holy Spirit's guidance. When God speaks to you, doubt says, "No, don't do that. You don't have the time, or the money, or the talent."

Unfortunately, the help the Lord just gave you would have opened up a great opportunity in your life or someone else's. But you couldn't hear His voice because He spoke into a heart full of thorns. Worry and doubt keep Him from producing good fruit in your life.

Take time to stop and listen to the voice of God. Follow His instructions. You will not only improve your life, but you will also be in a position to help others. Then you might overhear the Holy Spirit as He turns to Jesus and says, "Look at this heart of gold!"

A SERVANT'S HEART

Let's Pray.

Father, in the name of Jesus, we choose to listen to what You are saying to us. We will not be consumed with the cares of this world. We know that You are able to take care of us and that You will also care for others through us. We call for Your presence in our daily lives, Lord, and desire to be vessels of honor for Your glory. In Jesus' name, amen.

What Is to Come?

ACH MORNING BEGINS WITH a question: "I wonder what today will bring?"

Our culture pays palm readers and devours horoscopes to find out what is to come. We search out seers, mediums and psychics to find out what the future holds. We seek interpreters to find out what our dreams mean.

The world has provided a great mixture of answers, something to whet everyone's appetite. It's just like when you are craving a big, juicy cheeseburger. If you can't have one, you will try to fill the void with some other food. But even when your stomach is full, your cheeseburger craving remains unsatisfied.

Like a craving, eternal questions linger in your spirit, and you will look everywhere for the answers. If you search in the wrong places, the answers you find will never fully satisfy the truth you crave. Your mind may be full, but your heart will remain unsatisfied. Deep within your heart, you have the ability to distinguish wrong answers from the truth.

The Lord God holds your dreams and your future in His hands. His is not trying to hide the truth from you, and it doesn't cost money to find the answers. He is waiting to have a relationship with you. He sits on the edge of His throne, waiting for your questions about the future. He is driven by love and filled with anticipation to see the plans He has for you fulfilled.

The Holy Spirit lives inside of you, and He patiently waits for you to turn to Him. All of the answers already reside within you. You will never be satisfied with any direction or plan for your life unless it comes from the heart of God. When you heed His counsel for your day, you won't hunger for answers anymore. You'll be full of His vision.

A Servant's Heart

Let's Pray.

Father, in the name of Jesus, from this day forward, we will seek You every day. We will come to You first and seek Your plans for our future. When we ask You the meaning of our dreams, we know that You will answer. We know we will not be hungry for false counsel because Your answers satisfy our souls. We love You, and we want a personal relationship with You. In Jesus' name, amen.

If you would like to receive Jesus as your personal Savior, pray this prayer, and get in touch with someone you know who serves the Lord.

Salvation Prayer:

Jesus, please come into my heart. I give my life to You. Amen.

Be blessed in His love.

Are Things Going Wrong?

THERE ARE TIMES WHEN it seems like we are swimming in the pain of disappointment. Even when we stand on the promises and the character of God and follow the leading of the Holy Spirit, things seem to go wrong. When that happens, it feels like everyone is watching you, like you're living in a fishbowl, a sea of transparency.

There is no escaping the whispers, as people open their mouths wide with opinions. They gather at the dinner table, the water cooler, the telephone, and they talk about your life, reducing your disappointments to a mere conversation piece. You hear the voices saying, "Now isn't that a pity."

Jesus knows this road better than anyone. He left His seat in the heavenlies and walked away from the throne of glory. He took on an earthly body and relied solely on the Holy Spirit for guidance. He had one shot at His mission. If He failed, then He would lose the world. He would lose it all. He walked the Earth for 33 years, and the Father called Him to begin His ministry at age 30.

At that moment, Jesus began actively fulfilling His purpose. He brought healing into the world and freed captives from demonic oppression. Jesus was a strong, prosperous, compassionate man. He gave all of Himself, and then He gave more. There was never a man like Him, nor will there ever be. He was a teacher, minister, friend and brother.

But the time came when Jesus had to face the music, "Love Hurts." He walked away from the most effective ministry ever birthed. He turned down the chance to sit on an earthly throne. He gave up His human rights to justice and life. He followed the Holy Spirit to the cross, and He trusted

Him. He was whipped, scourged and beaten beyond recognition. He cried out to His Father, "My God, my God, why hast thou forsaken me?" only to hear the jeering of the people as His words disappeared into the gray sky (Mark 15:34, KJV).

"If thou be the Christ, save thyself" they mocked (Luke 23:39, KJV).

He could picture the setting, as people went home that day and sat around their tables, discussing what a pity it was about Jesus. "He could have really made something of Himself."

"Gosh, He had so much going for Him. He had such a great ministry, and He would have made a great leader."

"But He had to go another way. You know Jesus— such an extremist. And now look at Him, He lost it all."

Then they moved on to the next piece of news, as they wiped their mouths, dripping with gossip.

More than you can imagine, Jesus understands what it means to suffer as a result of obedience to God. He also knows the great faith it takes to trust the Holy Spirit through it all. But best of all, He understands that what looks like defeat in the eyes of men may bring great promotion in Heaven.

Let the people jeer, whisper and gossip, because you know the end of Jesus' story. He is the King of Kings and Lord of lords, and His name is above every name in Heaven and on Earth (Revelation 19:16; Philippians 2:9-10). He obeyed the Father's will over man's counsel, and He was greatly promoted!

I can't wait! How about you?

Let's Pray.

Father, we ask in the name of Jesus for continual guidance throughout our day. Amen

Without Honor

H AVE YOU EVER GONE from a position of honor to a new place where you are not accepted?

You did all the right things at home and at work. You lived your life as an example for your family, friends and neighbors. You prayed, worshipped and walked in love. You were as obedient to the Lord as you could possibly be. And you were honored by everyone you touched.

But then, God instructed you to share His ways in a new place.

You have obeyed Him in this many times. This has been your life, listening to and following His instructions, and as you have followed His lead, things have always fallen into place. The fruits of your labor surrounded you. People welcomed your presence and accepted your ideas. Life was good, and you told yourself, "See! All people have to do is follow God's voice, and everything will be great!"

But the next time, even though you did all the right things, the doors just didn't open. Your popularity and acceptance vanished, and you were rejected. Instead of peace and joy, your presence seemed to bring out the porcupine in everyone.

All you have left are memories from the past, which you cling to just to get through the long days. You go home, and as you kick off your shoes, you look at your dog and realize that "man's best friend" has taken on a very real meaning.

The Lord Jesus Himself endured this very scenario. He traveled through the land, and His fame was so great that at one point He had to get in a boat and teach from the water in order for everyone to see and hear Him.

With as much popularity and adoration as Jesus had, we would assume that He would always be embraced with honor. But one night as He prayed, the Holy Spirit told Jesus to go back to His homeland to preach, so He did. But this time, although the people were astonished at His wisdom, they were overcome by the fact that He was just one of them. They said to one another, " 'Where did this Man get these things? And what wisdom is this which is given to Him, that such mighty works are performed by His hands! Is this not the carpenter, the Son of Mary, and brother of James, Joses, Judas, and Simon? And are not His sisters here with us?' So they were offended at Him" (Mark 6:2-3, NKJV).

Jesus quickly discovered that the same good news that healed, saved and delivered the world could not help His own hometown because of their doubt. And He marveled! Jesus was not accepted by His own people, but the Lord sent Him there anyway.

So, understand that you may not receive honor in every place where the Lord leads you. But do not judge your current success based on others' acceptance. God sent you there knowing that the quills on a few backs would stand up. He gave you the Comforter, His Holy Spirit, to give you wisdom in those times. His ways and His thoughts are much higher than ours (Isaiah 55:11).

Don't judge your life based on anything but the Word of God. You will live through times of difficulty and times of great happiness. Be ready for both, and rejoice in Him through it all— not *for* the tough times, but *through* them.

If you are following His voice, then you will remain in His presence all the time. Isn't that what we want more than anything? To be in His presence? You can, if you follow His voice.

And it is there that you will always be honored!

A SERVANT'S HEART

Let's Pray.

Father, in the name of Jesus, we long to know You and to do Your will. We will follow You to the ends of the Earth to remain in Your precious, powerful presence. We only desire to be honored by You, not to receive the approval of others. In Jesus' name, amen.

Shhhhh!

HAVE YOU EVER BEEN in a situation when you were told to stay still and be quiet? For whatever reason, the surroundings needed to stay calm. All you had to do was leave everyone alone and mind your own business. People said, "We don't need any change here!" Look, we're doing great!" "Don't rock the boat!"

But that's exactly what Jesus wants us to do.

The Word of God says that Jesus had instructed His disciples to sail across the sea while He stayed ashore to pray. He saw them struggling to row against the wind and "would have passed them by", but the disciples cried out to Him (Mark 6:48-49, NKJV).

Jesus wasn't even going to stop talk to His friends as He walked across the water. He had a mission, and at that moment, it was to get to the other side.

When they left Him behind, the disciples probably assumed that He would be away for a day or so. So imagine, as they rowed, when all of a sudden something caught their attention. They stopped and squinted out into the sea. Was the fog playing tricks on their eyes? No, it wasn't fog, and it was coming towards them. A man.

Jesus wasn't their first guess; "when the disciples saw Him walking on the sea, they were troubled, saying, 'It is a ghost!' And they cried out for fear" (Matthew 14:26, NKJV).

But the Bible says that "immediately" when Jesus heard their fearful cry, He called out, "Be of good cheer! It is I; do not be afraid" (v. 27, NKJV).

Then Peter, in a strange and admirable act of faith, replied, "Lord, if it is You, command me to come to You on the water" (v. 28, NKJV).

Imagine the joy in Jesus' heart when He said, "Come" (v. 29, NKJV). "Come on out of that boat, Peter, and walk with Me!"

And he did.

The others could have done the same thing, but they chose not to rock the boat. It seemed safer to stay in. This leap of faith was too great for them after such a short amount of time. **They settled for security, and in so doing, they missed out on the walk of a lifetime.**

After that, they would only get to ride on the wind at Peter's back, as he shared with them what it was like to walk on water. Their only adrenaline came from the lump of fear in their throats; they couldn't even imagine getting out of that boat.

But Jesus needs us to be the Peters of our day in our jobs, schools, homes and churches. He needs people who will not only rock the boat, but turn the whole thing upside down if it's His will.

Change will only enter the world one boat at a time. Don't settle for safe and secure. Jesus didn't come here and beat the devil so that we could settle in and become complacent and apathetic. Cry out to Him, or He will walk right past you to those who call out in faith, "Lord, if that's You, tell me to come with You!"

Get out there and dare to walk on the waters of change. Soar on the winds of greatness among the clouds of power. When you step out, you will follow Him into magnificent experiences. Then everyone will surround you, taking hold of your coattails as they listen to your stories, and you'll see the fear in their eyes and notice that yours is gone!

A Servant's Heart

Let's Pray.

Father, we want to be used by You in business, art, music and all that we do. Keep us from falling into a mindset where blending in is the goal. Make us world-changers so that we can bring glory to Your name. In Jesus' name, amen.

Rejoice

D O YOU REMEMBER A time when someone handed you a key and said, "It's all yours!" Whether it was a vehicle or a house, something happened when they handed you that key; an exchange took place. Suddenly you were in charge. You became empowered.

In the same way, Jesus gave us a key: a commission. He appointed seventy-two additional disciples and sent them out two-by-two to heal the sick and spread the word that "the kingdom of heaven is come" (Matthew 12:28, KJV). He empowered them to leave His side and take the good news throughout the Earth in **His name**.

The seventy-two came back with joy and said, "Lord, even the devils are subject unto us **through thy name**" (Luke 10:17, KJV, emphasis mine).

Jesus replied, "I saw Satan fall like lightning from heaven. Behold, I give you the **authority** to trample on serpents and scorpions, and over all the power of the enemy, and nothing shall by any means hurt you. Nevertheless do not rejoice in this... but rather rejoice because your names are written in heaven" (Luke 10:18-20, NKJV).

This is an example of the most powerful exchange in the history of the universe. Jesus gave us His name, His power and eternal life in Heaven, and we gave Him our shame, sin and disease. That makes me feel like rejoicing!

No matter where you are or what you've done or haven't done, the kingdom of Heaven is knocking at your door today! Open the door and say "Yes" to Jesus and the great exchange.

Let Him take over your life, and then tell everyone about Him everywhere you go. No matter what, you're in for eternity! That is definitely something to rejoice about.

A Servant's Heart

Let's Pray.

Father, we thank You for Jesus, for His blood and for the unfathomable gift of His life. We ask Jesus to come into our hearts right now. We want all that You have, and we give You all we that have and all we are. In Jesus' name, amen.

The Person Within

I was watching a movie recently, and when the hero was facing a monumental decision, he was reminded, "**With great power comes great responsibility.**" You could take a lifetime to unpack that statement, for we have all been created by the Master of the universe.

If you drive through a state park or walk through Sea World, it won't take you long to admire the beautiful creations of your Heavenly Father. But to trump all that, God made one special creation like Him and called it "man."

He made man beautiful, strong and intelligent. He breathed life into him. And then He gave man a gift, a dominion all our own to care for and rule over: Earth! And with this great gift, God entrusted us with great responsibility.

But tragically, we didn't trust Him. Instead, we believed the snake when he whispered, "God is lying! You are not powerful like Him." And we paid the price for our waywardness: We lost the Earth to Satan. Ever since that day, we have been on the move to reclaim lost ground.

The good news is, God didn't leave us alone in this ordeal; He sent Jesus to redeem us. God renewed our standing with Him through Christ's innocent blood. All our sins were forgiven, and we are new creatures in Christ Jesus. He gave us the authority of Jesus' name to stand against the devil and his cohorts, and He empowered us once again to govern the Earth.

And a second time, God instructed man to fill the Earth: "Go into all the world and preach the gospel to every creature" (Mark 16:15, NKJV). "Tell everyone that **once again**, all things are possible for those who believe Him!" (Matthew 19:26).

Will we make the same mistake twice?

You have been given great and mighty gifts! You are beautiful, strong and intelligent. You are a child of the most high God! Whether you are a mother, father, boss, friend, teacher, student, artist, singer, actor— you name it— your life is a gift.

Stop making excuses about how you're not-so-important, or why you can't do something. You are doing the same thing Adam did: telling your Father that He didn't make you as magnificent as He intended. I wouldn't want to stand up to my own family and say that about myself, let alone God!

You have to be pretty brave to tell Him that He made you insignificant. His Word says, "And God saw **every thing** that he had made, and, behold, it was **very** good" (Genesis 1:31, KJV, emphasis mine).

I will ask you a question and leave it at that: Is God lying, or are you?

I will leave you with Him now, as He patiently awaits your response. He gives you the ability to fulfill your purpose on Earth. Reign with Him in it!

Your **response** unlocks your God-given **ability**.

A SERVANT'S HEART

Have a blessed day in Him!

Let's Pray.

Father, in the name of Jesus we ask for the strength and courage to become more like Jesus. Amen

A Key's Design

THERE'S NOTHING LIKE COMING home after a long day at work with a bag of groceries in one arm and a baby in the other. You shuffle for the right key, slide it into the keyhole and try to turn it, but you don't hear the familiar "click," and the key doesn't budge. You twist it again, and still nothing happens. You pull it out and realize that it's the wrong one.

You fumble through your keys again and slide the right key into the keyhole; the door opens and you're in. Your other keys look similar, but they don't match the cut of the keyhole, so they can't unlock the door.

Think about all the doors in the world— that's a lot of keys!

There are **many** doors in the kingdom of Heaven as well, and behind those doors are blessings. There are abundant opportunities, talents, gifts, healings and much more, but it is our responsibility to use the right key to unlock the door in every situation.

In the Gospel of Mark, Jesus was speaking of having faith in God, and He said, "whoever **says to this mountain** [or situation], 'Be removed and be cast into the sea,' and **does not doubt** in his heart, but believes that those things he says will be done; he will have whatever he says" (Mark 11:23, KJV).

Essentially, Jesus was saying that even the most seemingly impossible situation is a door, and the key that unlocks it is **faith spoken without doubt**. When you speak to your circumstances and believe what you say in your heart, then what you say will be done! But if you speak negatively about your situation, there will be no change.

Jesus went on to say, "Therefore I say to you, whatever things **you ask when you pray, believe that you receive them**, and you will have them" (Mark 11:24, NKJV).

Here, Jesus gave us the key to another door: **When you pray, believe that God will give you what you ask Him for, and you will receive it!**

In His next breath, Jesus emphasized the importance of forgiveness: "And whenever you stand praying, if you have anything against anyone, forgive him" (Mark 11:25, NKJV).

This is yet another key— one that unlocks God's forgiveness towards you. Forgiveness heals your heart and brings joy, and it causes a domino effect in the rest of your life. **You will live, love and laugh. Blessings from Heaven will be able to flow freely into your heart.**

There are many doors in the kingdom of Heaven, and many keys to unlock them. If your door isn't opening, take a look; you might be using the wrong key.

You may ask, "How will I know which key to use?"

Ask your Father. It's *His* kingdom, and He will gladly show you! After all, the kingdom was prepared for **you**!

A SERVANT'S HEART

Let's Pray.

Father, we ask you to show us the keys that correspond to every situation in our lives. Your Word says that whatever we ask You for, You will give us. We seek You for the answers to every problem and every endeavor. Thank You, Lord. In Jesus' name, amen.

Prayer and Fasting

ONE OF THE MAIN reasons that we fast and pray is so that we can hear and follow the direction of the Lord.

There are many types of fasting. You can fast from food, sports or entertainment. Fasting is a way to instill discipline and self-control in your life. It is very rewarding. When you set boundaries for yourself, you realize that your spirit is stronger than your body, and you feel empowered.

But more importantly, fasting and prayer open avenues for you to draw closer to the Holy Spirit. Fasting is a way to minimize the distractions in your life so that you can focus more of your attention on the Lord. The object of your focus always becomes the biggest, most important thing in your life; let God occupy that position.

Jesus gave us an example of the power of prayer and fasting. After the Transfiguration, He approached His disciples and saw the scribes disputing with them. Jesus walked up to the scribes and asked, "What are you discussing with them?" (Mark 9:16, NKJV).

A man in the crowd stepped forward and explained, "Teacher, I brought You my son, who has a mute spirit. And wherever it seizes him, it throws him down; he foams at the mouth, gnashes his teeth, and becomes rigid. So I spoke to Your disciples, that they should cast it out, but they could not" (vv. 17-18).

Jesus replied, "O faithless generation, how long shall I be with you? How long shall I bear with you? Bring him to Me" (v. 19).

Jesus had spent much time teaching His disciples what to do and how to do it, yet they still didn't walk in the power that He had given them. They still couldn't heal the sick, cast out demons or raise the dead. At that moment, He probably thought, "Will they ever learn?!" He expected them to be able to walk in the same power that He did, but they lacked the faith to do so.

After a brief, compassionate conversation with the boy's father, Jesus confronted the spirit, saying, "Deaf and dumb spirit, I command you, **come out** of him and enter him no more!" (v. 25, emphasis mine).

The spirit immediately left, and the boy was set free. Jesus helped him up, and he was completely normal.

Later, Jesus' disciples asked Him privately, "Why couldn't we cast it out?"

Jesus replied, "This kind can come out by nothing but prayer and fasting" (v. 29).

So you see, prayer and fasting are important parts of the Christian life. Not only will they bring you closer to the Holy Spirit, you will begin to understand the heart of God and walk in His power.

Jesus implied that fasting and prayer were a regular part of His life. This no doubt enabled Him to remain all the more attentive to the Holy Spirit so that He was able to do what He saw His Father doing wherever He went.

That is the importance of praying to get the direction from the Lord. It is wise to fast and pray about business decisions, whether you're weighing investments, teaching children or treating patients. God desires for you to walk in His power in everything you do. He wants you to be an awesome example of His glory in this Earth. He wants to release His power into everything you touch.

When you fast and pray, spend more time with an open heart and a closed mouth, and listen to the Holy Spirit. You will find that He gives you crystal-clear direction and mighty power!

A SERVANT'S HEART

Let's Pray.

Father, we will fast and pray before You. We want to draw near to You and to hear the Holy Spirit's direction in every area of our lives. We ask You for creative ideas, answers to problems and power to change lives, and we thank You for it. In Jesus' name, amen.

I See You

DO YOU REMEMBER WHEN you first realized that you had an inner voice? A deep sense of purpose or a desire to dream beyond your surroundings? The voice would speak to you at any given moment, whether you were in a crowd or all alone, "Why don't I fit in? Why do I feel like I have a special purpose in life?"

You go through life asking the inner question, "Does anyone see me?"

Jesus was in the same situation when He walked the Earth as a man, and He had a purpose to fulfill *as a man*. His destiny was great, but His road was rough. He lived 30 years before He began actively fulfilling that purpose. Although He was born with His future already decided, it took years for it to develop. But when He reached the age of 33, the Father finally said, "Jesus, it is time."

And Jesus started His ministry, traveling across the country, preaching and teaching. Then He came to a point when all of His disciples were in place, and He was training them to take over the ministry when He left. Jesus knew that He had a great mission to accomplish and that He would die to save all mankind. But for quite some time, He was alone in His understanding of the big picture. As He walked and talked with His disciples, He wondered, "Do they see Me? Do they know who I really am?"

So one day, while Jesus was with His disciples, He asked them that very question:

Whom do men say that I the Son of man am?

And they said, Some say that thou art John the Baptist: some, Elias; and others, Jeremias, or one of the prophets (Matthew 16:13-14, KJV).

They were assuring Jesus that the people thought He was very important, but what He really wanted to know was who *they* thought He was. He replied, "But whom say **ye** that I am?" (v. 15).

In other words, Jesus was saying, "Do you really see Me?"

And in a moment of sudden boldness, Peter answered, "Thou art the Christ, the Son of the living God" (v. 16).

There it was: For the first time in His life, someone saw Jesus for who He really was. This gave Him a boost of confidence in Himself, His friends and His Heavenly Father. From that point on, He could share all of His revelations, His heart and the things that were about to take place.

When someone comes along and speaks into your life, confirming what the Lord has been speaking to you since you were a child, be assured that they see *you*! This is a God-inspired confirmation and a release for you to move forward in faith. It is an open door and a boost of confidence in yourself, other people and God.

God has placed a purpose within you. Take that purpose, set your face like flint, and move in that direction! Don't Stop. I see you!

A Servant's Heart

Let's Pray.

Father, we thank You for Your purpose in each of our lives. We will focus all of our attention in that direction to fulfill what You have called us to accomplish. In Jesus' name, amen.

Have a blessed day in Him!

Show Me a Sign!

AVE YOU EVER KNOWN someone who was never satisfied, no matter how much you did for them? You lavish praise on them, buy them gifts and spend as much time with them as you can, yet you walk away knowing that they will soon feel entitled to more. They return to you with the underlying notion that you have fallen short of your duty to their life. You are made to feel like you didn't do or give enough, but you know that you have given all you have.

This is a very frustrating situation. You dig deep and confront the silent voice of control and manipulation with an unspoken decision: "I don't have to prove anything to you."

Don't feel alone; isolation is one of Satan's most effective ways of controlling you. If he can get you to chase your tail, then he knows you will remain in a crippling tail-spin for the rest of your life— out of his way so that you won't confront him with holy power that lives within you.

Jesus was in the same predicament. He went about, healing the sick, feeding thousands of people with a few loaves of bread, setting captives free. Everything He did was motivated by a giving heart. He prayed for the people, walked with them, talked with them and ate with them. At times He would fast and go up into the mountains to pray while His disciples rested. He loved them, and you could tell.

And yet the Word says, "Then the Pharisees and the Sadducees came, and **tempting** him asked that He would **show them** a sign from heaven" (Matthew 16:1, NKJV, emphasis mine).

Even John the Baptist sent men to ask Jesus, "Art thou he that should come, or do we look for another?" (Matthew 11:3, KJV).

The purpose of John's ministry was to prepare the way for the Messiah who would save us from our sins, and for a time, everything was going great. Thousands were flocking into the desert just to hear what he had to say about the One to come. He preached a bold message with an anointed voice and power behind his words.

But after he baptized Jesus, trouble came, and John was arrested for opening his mouth on a particular subject. There he was, in jail, and the crowds stayed far away from him. He lost his insight and sense of purpose, and he began to look at Jesus with questions in his heart. He was focusing on himself, and he wondered if Jesus even cared about his plight.

So John decided to send two of his friends to ask Jesus, "Are you really the Christ?"

This was an outlet for John's silent voice which shouted, "What about me? Don't You care about me? Prove to me that You love me!"

John, not unlike the Pharisees, was asking Jesus to prove Himself in order to satisfy his insecurity, rather than trusting Jesus' ministry.

The Pharisees tried to manipulate and control Jesus' ministry. Had He yielded to their maneuvers, Jesus would have jeopardized His calling, and today we might not be able to say, "By His stripes we are healed, and our sins have been forgiven by the blood of the Lamb."

You have a powerful purpose within you, and Satan knows it. He will try to break your focus by causing you to doubt God's ways. If you allow this type of control, you will be perpetually trying to prove to someone that you really do care. Don't fall into this trap or be a trap for someone else in this way. Be strong, focused and full of courage. Know that you are loved and significant in Jesus' eyes.

A SERVANT'S HEART

Let's Pray.

Father, we worship You and give You all the glory. We will focus on Your purpose for our lives and fulfill what You have called us to do. We receive the Spirit's wisdom and power. We love You. In Jesus' name, amen.

Have a blessed day!

If the Stripes Could Talk

I WAS CLEANING OUT MY basement the other day, and I came across an old American flag that was battered and worn from hanging outside. I stopped what I was doing and found myself staring at it. Then I heard the Holy Spirit ask me a question. He said, "When you look at the flag, do you see life, or do you see death?"

It was a profound moment. I suddenly saw the people who died so that the rest of us could live. I answered, "I see both life and death when I look at the flag."

As I held it, I heard Him say, "**If the stripes could talk…**"

I felt the heartbeat of every person who has served or is serving our country. Thousands of voices seemed to rise from its red stripes. I felt their pain, strength and sacrifice. I felt love. Then the Holy Spirit said, "Just like that flag which hangs from buildings and homes, blowing with every gust of wind, God hears thousands of voices saying, "We have paid the price for you. Our blood was shed, and we gave our freedom for you."

Jesus, too, gave His life for the world. He died for us so that we could have eternal life. He was beaten and whipped 39 times, and each stroke left a stripe of torn flesh bleeding on His back. With every stripe Jesus took, the voice of God says, "**By His stripes, you were healed**."

"For God so loved the world that he gave his one and only Son, that whoever believes in him shall not perish but have eternal life" (John 3:16, NIV).

And so, we give our lives to Him. We become the voices in His stripes, crying out as one as we reach out to the nations and tell them the great price He paid for them. Our voices now rise from His stripes, saying, "Thank you, Jesus, for paying the price— Your blood— for my life."

Our voices rise up as one to God our Father. They stretch across the sky over the world like a flag waving, "Freedom! Salvation!" But our flag can't be hung on a pole or building. It is embedded on the back of Jesus. Every stripe is still there.

Now, when you look at the American flag, think of Jesus. I ask you, **Can you hear the stripes talk?**

A Servant's Heart

Let's Pray.

Father, we thank You for the stripes on Jesus' back. Without them, we would not have life. Thank You for the flag and that, with every star and stripe, we can know the worth of the freedom given to us. We worship You and give You glory. In Jesus' name, amen.

Have a blessed day!

Mentors

EVERYONE NEEDS A MENTOR. If you don't learn from someone who knows more than you, how can you grow?

Jesus assigned 72 disciples to go out two by two. We are not meant to face the world alone. The Bible advises us not to forsake the assembling of ourselves together (Hebrews 10:25).

Church— that is, fellowship with fellow believers— encourages accountability and provides a safety net. When you branch off alone, you might end up taking a side road without even noticing. Right seems wrong, and wrong seems right.

You ask, "How will I know?"

I have experienced this first-hand. My relationship with the Lord was strong and healthy, but, for several reasons, I ended up in a place where I was unable to be a part of a strong church.

Down the road, I made some compromises, and my life began to decay. I quickly turned my attention to finding a strong church, and I have not turned back. Godly leadership acts as a covering for my life just like an umbrella in the rain. Not only do I learn much about Jesus and myself, I have friends of all ages. Some I learn from, and some learn from me.

Being unable to learn from people or having difficulty submitting to authority is a red flag in your life. Take a look at yourself. Who is your mentor? If you don't have one, ask God to help you find a great woman or man of God to learn from. Get involved in a strong church and learn to serve. You may have to learn that things don't always have to go your way, but this will bring tremendous growth in your life.

If Jesus surrounded Himself with twelve disciples and asked them to pray for Him, then I think we should do the same. There is strength in numbers.

A Servant's Heart

Have a blessed day!

Let's Pray.

Father, we ask in Jesus name for people you have chosen for us to be placed in our lives daily. Amen

Within Lies the Future

T HE SECRET TO FULFILLING your dreams and obtaining your goals is the refusal to quit.

Everyone has a voice within that either says, "I can," or, "I can't."

The only difference between a champion and everyone else is that a champion chooses to listen to the positive voice and tune out the negative.

Inadequacy is an emotion, not a fact. You must refuse to believe the voice of discouragement and move forward one step at a time.

Everything starts by taking just one step. Success ends when forward motion ceases.

A SERVANT'S HEART

Let's Pray.

Father, we worship You today. We give You glory, honor and praise. Holy Spirit, use us for Your purpose. Accomplish what You have called us to do in our lifetime. We say "Yes" to that purpose. We will walk with You, one step at a time. In Jesus' name, amen.

But ye, beloved, [build] up yourselves on you most holy faith, praying in the Holy Ghost" (Jude 1:20, KJV).

New Tongues

JESUS DIED FOR OUR sins, and when we accept Him as our personal Savior, we gain the assurance of eternal life in Heaven. But in His death, we also gained new life in this age. We were recreated and reborn, and everything about us became brand-new.

When you were a baby, you learned to talk. Words are one of your most effective vehicles on the Earth. You can tell where you are and where you will end up by listening to yourself talk.

Until Jesus came, we didn't have power over our words. Humanity was under a curse, and death reigned over our tongues. But Jesus redeemed us from the curse when He fulfilled the Law. We now have control over our conversations.

We were given a new way to speak.

Like children, we have to learn all over again how to use our words effectively.

Jesus said, "they shall speak with new tongues" (Mark 16:17, KJV).

Not other tongues, *new* tongues. He taught His disciples that with their new ability to **control** their own speech, they could "cast out devils" in His name (v. 17). They could now live with power generated by the engines of their mouths.

Re-train yourself in conversation. The words you speak directly affect your future. God gave you the power: "Death and life are in the power of the tongue" (Proverbs 18:21, KJV).

It's up to you. Where is your speech taking you?

A SERVANT'S HEART

Make it a blessed day in the Lord!

Let's Pray.

Father, in the name of Jesus we thank you for the wisdom to know your voice and to follow you all the days of our lives. Amen

From Glory to Glory

WHAT DO YOUR PLANS for the future sound like? *Get a good job, get married, have children*— If that's a picture of your life, then I would say it's pretty drab. You were made to live from glory to glory. **We are to live today** with everything we have.

We need to press for more of God's power and presence so that we can experience **extreme joy, extreme peace and extreme power!** We are to laugh, cry, run and jump! **Our joy comes from living in the presence of the Lord**. Our bad days can be more full of joy than the best days of those who don't know Him.

Isn't that great news? The devil is furious about that, and I want him to know how glad I am that he's mad! He wants us to walk with lead in our feet and iron in our hearts. He wants us depressed— gloomy about life.

But we need to get up every day and fight for our God-given right to have fun. Cast aside everything you are going through, and start laughing aloud in the air, declaring, "I'm going to have fun today!" No matter what bills wait on the counter top, what the doctor has said, or how awful the weather is, go look in the mirror and realize that this is your life! You only have one shot at it, so give it your all.

We can live in God's glory now, and when we take our last earthly breath, we will step out of our bodies and into the presence and glory of the Lord.

Realize that circumstances cannot control you if you don't let them. Whatever fills your heart will shape your life day by day. A change of heart can change your whole worldview!

A SERVANT'S HEART

Make a joyful noise unto the Lord, all ye lands.

Serve the Lord with gladness: come before his presence with singing.

Know ye not that the Lord he is God: it is he that hath made us, and not we ourselves; we are his people, and the sheep of his pasture.

Enter into his gates with thanksgiving, and into his courts with praise: be thankful unto him, and bless his name.

For the Lord is good; his mercy is everlasting; and his truth endureth to all generations (Psalm 100).

Have a blessed day!

Let's Pray.

Father, in the name of Jesus we thank you for your love every day. Amen

Simplicity and Greatness

S ATAN WHISPERS INTO THE ears of a hundred generations, "How dare you take the all the power and glory of the kingdom of God and bring it to Earth, as if it is yours!"

He lurks in the shadows, sneering, "They cannot, they will not, because I have deceived them all. I have convinced them that they are worthless and useless— too weak and unworthy for God's kingdom."

What Satan doesn't want you to know is this: **God's truth is simple.** Its **simplicity** is what makes it so gloriously pure. It is crystal clear, easy to carry, free of burden. It is also deeply peaceful. Yet our physical bodies cannot contain its power.

Jesus said, "I am the way, the **truth**, and the life" (John 14:6, KJV). He is the **power!**

But Satan only has to focus on one thing to keep us from realizing the power and authority that has been given to us from the beginning: **He distorted the truth!** Why? Because, **in truth lies the power of God**. Truth is God. It is His presence. It gives life and anointing. Truth is the Tree of Life.

Jesus came with simplicity, and He taught His disciples to walk in the power that had redeemed them. This is what made the Pharisees so angry. If it was so simple for people to experience God's power and presence, then their lives were meaningless. If God's kingdom was built on truth, and everyone could freely access His love, then there would be no need for the Law and, consequently, their esteemed positions. The heavy yoke they put upon the people would be rendered unnecessary. The Pharisees wanted to believe that the power of God was only for a prestigious, holy few. This secured their positions in life.

But Jesus contradicted all of that. He said, "my yoke is easy, and my burden is light" (Matthew 11:30, KJV). He walked the streets, He walked on water, He raised the dead. And then He said, "You, too, can go and do these things in My name" (see John 14:12).

His only requirement is faith— that we allow the truth to carry us through the woven web of man's thinking. Truth is raining down from the heavenlies, trying to break through our habitual doubt. Truth calls to anyone who will listen, "I am simple, I am power, I am perfect."

A Servant's Heart

I see it now. The Spirit of Truth is here in my room and resting in my yard. I can feel the sensational power of total peace; it is an exhilarating sensation in my bones. It is too sweet for words.

I can see Truth as both a Man and an atmosphere at the same time. I hope He is here to stay; I don't want to lose this moment. I long for these moments, and when I'm in them, I never want to leave.

Jesus, I love you. We are so free.

I can see the hardship and legalism that Satan has given us to hide the simplicity of the truth **because therein lies the power of the anointing**.

Holy Spirit, please don't let us lose sight of this. Take us deeper in Your truth, and teach us how to walk in it. We want to bring it to all people, in Jesus' name.

Watch and Pray

Jesus said, "Watch and pray, lest you enter into temptation" (Mark 14:38, NKJV).

We sometimes see temptation as a lust of our flesh, like drinking, stealing or gossiping, but that's not what Jesus was trying to convey when He spoke that warning. Jesus told His disciples to watch and pray because following God's will sometimes feels like walking down the wrong road. Things don't go like we expect. Days seem short; nights seem long. Roadblocks pop up everywhere we turn as if to box us in.

And then the **ultimate temptation** drifts into our minds as scent follows a rose. A voice pounding in your head, saying, *What if...?*

What if I had chosen a different road? Maybe I wouldn't be in this painful situation.

Jesus looked long and hard at that same tempting thought. He knelt in the Garden of Gethsemane, completely alone, the painful end looming in His immediate future. He knew His purpose, though His friends and family were certain that it was the wrong road. Even Peter, His rock, had tried to stop Him from choosing the road of selflessness, but Jesus had harshly rebuked Him: "Get behind Me, Satan!" (Matthew 16:23, NKJV).

As He prayed in the garden that night, perhaps Jesus reflected back on Peter's loving words, drawing strength from that moment to carry on. He asked His Heavenly Father, "if it is possible, let this cup pass from Me; nevertheless, not as I will, but as You will" (Matthew 26:39, NKJV).

That day probably went by too fast, but Jesus' sleepless night in the garden was long. The tempting voice of His enemy haunted His thoughts. *What if this is the wrong road? Don't do this; the price is too high. It's not worth it. There must be another way.*

But Jesus kept His eyes on the prize, not on Himself. And we, the very ones who were sending Him to His torturous death, were the prize. Can you imagine? He trusted the path that the Father had laid out for Him, knowing that it would lead to a far better outcome than any other He would choose.

So He went on to His death.

And now, the name of Jesus is **far above every name in Heaven and Earth** (see Philippians 2:9-10).

So if your days are short and your nights drag on, if it feels like the walls are closing in, if doubt tempts you to question God's direction, if you feel like throwing in the towel, **watch and pray**! Ask the Holy Spirit to help you keep your eyes on Jesus and His great purpose for your existence.

Pressure often indicates that you are on the right road, God's path. He has given you the power to outrun and overcome your enemy. You will be praised at Heaven's gates for your perseverance, having fulfilled the will of God!

A Servant's Heart

Have a blessed day in Him!

Let's Pray.

Father, in the name of Jesus we thank you for giving us boldness to take on all that you called us to do. Amen

The Black Day

O N THE SLEEPLESS NIGHT when His last day began, Jesus was on His knees, calling out to His Father, "if it is Your will, take this cup away from Me; nevertheless not My will, but Yours, be done" (Luke 22:42, NKJV).

In the middle of the night, He embraced His fate with great anticipation over the day to come. The sun would not shine for Him, nor would He hear the birds sing. He could already feel the pain of His obedience, but He trusted the Holy Spirit, who led Him to this place. Not to a bright, crisp morning, but to a dark night that Jesus knew would turn to a black day.

God had a mighty plan for Him and for the world. Jesus had only to endure this last day, for He knew then that the Master's plan would change the course of eternity.

But alone, Jesus had to bear the punishment for all the sins of the world. Only the mythical Atlas, who was said to forever carry the world on his shoulders, could possibly conceive of His burden.

Jesus knew that the time had come when the day would seem no brighter than the night. Black to black. And so, the Light walked into the valley of the shadow of death.

Jesus **trusted the Father in His time of distress.** Now the Father asks this question: **Will you?**

A Servant's Heart

Let's Pray.

Holy Spirit, we ask You to help us turn all of our problems over to You. When we pray, help us to trust You to meet our needs. In Jesus' name, amen.

Poem

Something doesn't feel right anymore.

Things have changed. Can't go back.

It is one of those moments when everything is so near.

Looking into the past, I know I am not there.

Looking into the future, things are unclear,

Like looking into a clouded crystal ball.

Lord, tell me what is to come.

Give me the courage to persevere, oh Lord.

Give me the strength to walk one more step.

The day is drawn, and the evening gone.

I wake up tomorrow and say, "What have I done?"

"Will I have made a difference once I'm gone?"

Lord, keep me from feeling satisfied.

Keep me always wanting more, wanting to go forward.

Don't let me see my future.

Thank You for the courage to persevere and the strength to go on.

The day is gone and the evening set.

I wake up tomorrow and say, "Look at what I have done."

"I've made a difference, and now I'm gone."

My past, present and future are complete.

And I have You always to seek.

You are enough, my King, you are my ring.

Amen.

A Servant's Heart

His head is as the most fine gold, his locks are bushy, and black as a raven.

His eyes are as the eyes of doves by the rivers of waters, washed with milk, and fitly set.

His cheeks are as a bed of spices, as sweet flowers: his lips like lilies, dropping sweet smelling myrrh.

His hands are as gold rings set with the beryl: his belly is as bright ivory overlaid with sapphires.

His legs are as pillars of marble, set upon sockets of fine gold: his countenance is as Lebanon, excellent as the cedars.

His mouth is most sweet: yea, he is altogether lovely. This is my beloved, and this my friend, O daughters of Jerusalem (Solomon 5:11-16, KJV).

The Kingdom of God

D O YOU LONG FOR the day when Jesus returns, riding on the wings of the wind as our King of kings? Ah, yes. It is a day many generations have dreamed of. One day, this will all be over. All we really have to do is wait, right?

Wrong! As Jesus was passing through Jericho on His way to Jerusalem, He told His disciples that "the Son of Man has come to seek and to save that which was lost" (Luke 19:10, NKJV).

The disciples thought Jesus was saying that the kingdom of God would immediately appear as Jesus worked, but that's not what He meant. He was teaching them that they should "**Occupy**" this world until He returns (see Luke 19:13 KJV). Jesus also said, "Go into all the world... In My name" (Mark 16:15, 17, NKJV). His name carries the authority to move mountains with a word. Jesus was directing them and us to **rule over the Earth**.

Occupy and multiply! Consider a garden. Tiny seedlings are planted, and then the garden becomes a battleground between the seedlings and the weeds. Either the weeds are removed, or the new plants are choked out. And what is the point? **The remaining plants occupy the ground**.

This is how the kingdom of God will appear. It won't happen all of a sudden, like a curtain dropping down in a theater at intermission that is then lifted to reveal a brand-new world for us to occupy. It isn't like we can sit back and eat popcorn, watching the events unfold like a play, waiting for the Lord to return. No. We have a **major** role to fulfill on stage before the kingdom of God can appear.

It won't be immediate. His kingdom appears here and there every time we reclaim more ground for Him on Earth, as we spread His presence throughout this world, winning souls, sharing the gospel. As the church grows and multiplies, the kingdom of God appears. Like a garden, we will become the dominant plant occupying the ground, choking out the weeds.

When the Groom returns for His bride, the church, we will have the Earth to present to Him as our wedding gift! We are waiting for our new day, but He is waiting on us to bring it!

A SERVANT'S HEART

Let's Pray.

Father, in the name of Jesus, awaken us to claim all ground for You and Your glory. Give us wisdom, Lord, to go into all the Earth and become who You have called us to be with boldness and courage. In Jesus' name, amen.

Are You Wired?

"SHE'S WIRED!"

What does that phrase mean? It implies that the individual has a high energy level, like an electrical system. One wire running through a wall provides electric connections, called outlets. When wired correctly, anything with a plug can be plugged into any outlet, and power will run through it. It doesn't matter what it is, how big it is, or what color. If it is plugged in, then it will have power.

God the Father is the source of power, Jesus is the wire, and the Holy Spirit is the electricity. And you are the plug. When you tap into the power of God, you are plugging yourself into the **source of power**. It doesn't matter your gender, race, size or socioeconomic class. All you have to do is connect yourself to God, and you will walk in His redemption.

Power! Life! You will develop capabilities and deepen your capacity for the purpose God has given you, all a result of being plugged into the Source. He gives all of Himself to anyone who will give all of themselves to Him. The trade off is magnificent.

Whether you're praying for one person or thousands, the power runs through you, in the name of Jesus.

When you go to do something new, something that makes you feel uncomfortable, nervous, inadequate or afraid, concentrate on your relationship with God. Visualize yourself being plugged into the outlet, **who is your Father**, and know that He does the work **through you**.

Without you, how can God do anything? Satan doesn't want you to know this simple truth. He wants you to believe that you're not good enough, smart enough or strong enough. It's a lie! **God needs you to be a vessel** through which He can help others, and in turn, bless you.

Remember, you are a walking plug. Look at your life; what are you plugging into? That will directly determine what runs through you. Plug into the Father's power and life, and be wired!

A SERVANT'S HEART

Remember to reach out to someone today. The greatest way to defeat self pity is by reaching outward instead of inward!

"I am the vine, you are the branches" (John 15:5, NKJV).

Let's Pray.

Father, we ask in Jesus name for the Holy Spirit to continually lead us into your presence. Amen

Two Kinds of Wisdom

There are two kinds of wisdom:

> Godly wisdom: **"If any of you lacks wisdom, let him ask of God, who gives to all liberally** and without reproach, and it will be given to him" (James 1:5, NKJV, emphasis mine).

> Satan's wisdom: **"This wisdom does not descend from above, but is earthly, sensual, demonic"** (James 3:15, NKJV, emphasis mine).

Satan is the embodiment of death. Everything he does produces destruction. There is no other outcome when he is at the helm. He is the opposite of God in all things.

God is the path to life. His wisdom is the strong foundation upon which we should build our lives. When you ask the Lord for wisdom and direction in your life, He will give it to you. But from there, it is important to keep seeking His wisdom. You need it in order to stay on His path in your journey.

As a carpenter builds a house, he learns the best materials to use. If he chooses the wrong bonding materials, then the house will fall apart. **Like that carpenter, we not only need God's wisdom in our decisions, but we need the wisdom to keep it all together.**

If we lack the wisdom to maintain the relationships, jobs and finances God has given us, then we run the great risk of losing it all. And that is Satan's order: Gain it all, then lose it all. The key is to gain it and **keep it!** This is God's goal for us.

No one on Earth can teach us how to do this. Earthly wisdom cannot manage the blessings of God; that wisdom comes only from the Holy Spirit. **All you have to do is ask, listen and have patience**.

Jesus told the Parable of the Wheat and the Tares (weeds):

> The kingdom of heaven is like a man who sowed good seed in his field; but while men slept, his enemy came and sowed tares among the wheat and went his way. But when the grain had sprouted and produced a crop, then the tares also appeared. So the servants of the owner came and said to him… "Do you want us then to go and gather them up?" But he said, "No, lest while you gather up the tares you also uproot the wheat with them. Let both grow together until the harvest, and at the time of harvest I will say to the reapers, 'First gather together the tares and bind them in bundles to burn them, but gather the wheat into my barn' " (Matthew 13:24-30, NKJV).

That is wisdom! The wheat represents Christians living in the world. Satan is trying to tear us all out, leaving only destruction, confusion and death.

God is the Father of wisdom, and He has promised to give it all to you, without holding back! Just ask the Lord, not only for instruction and direction, but for the wisdom to maintain what He gives you. Choose daily which wisdom to build your life on.

A SERVANT'S HEART

Give someone a smile or a kind word today. They need you!

Let's Pray.

Father, in the name of Jesus we ask for your wisdom and direction daily for our lives. Amen

You Can Still Go

FROM THE MOMENT WE wake up in the morning until we finally lie down at night, most days don't seem to contain enough time for all of our plans. We rush to work and eat on the way. We eat lunch even faster because time is already running out. We drive home with the dinner plans on our minds, trying to decide if there is enough in the pantry to complete the meal. And tomorrow comes, day after day.

Then one day, we realize that the years have passed by, and the love we once had for the Lord seems to been lost in the routine. Oh, we still love Him, but where did the time go? It seems like only yesterday we were so close to Him, but now we only talk to God on the drive to work. We have been through so much with Him, and He was always there. How could we have gone so long with only a few moments to spare for Him?

It's okay, you can still go to Him. He's right there, and He is not mad at you. He still cares. He will never leave you nor forsake you, not in a million years. He is the Truth, the Life and the Way. He is always waiting for you and will embrace you whenever you come to Him.

The Lord is your Rock. He's your Strong Tower and your Safety Net.

He's the Light in the dark times and your Living Water in the dry times. He's your Healer and your Provider.

He holds the answer to all your problems, and He can create balance when everything seems out of line.

When you're ready, know that you can still go to Him. He is there, and He is waiting for you.

A SERVANT'S HEART

Have a blessed day.

Let's Pray.

Father, in the name of Jesus we thank you that you are our constant source of strength in our daily lives. Amen

Looking to See a Miracle

A**S YOU WERE DRIVING,** have you ever seen a homeless person pushing a cart full of stuff? All of their possessions in the world are probably in that cart. And then you realize what you have, and what they don't.

Suddenly, nagging the kids seems silly. Your spouse's expectations seem insignificant. You have a revelation, and you think to yourself, "That person needs a miracle. I wish they could experience a huge blessing, so they would feel as blessed as I do."

And then you continue to drive, and the person with the cart fades into the distance.

God doesn't just drop blessings from the sky. They come through us. At that moment, you could have blessed that person's life. Yes, you!

As you drove by that homeless person, and those thoughts went through your mind, you were the vessel God wanted to use to bless them. You were the blessing. And you can be the miracle in someone else's life today.

This isn't just about money; Jesus certainly didn't need cash to make someone's day. God chose you to serve others in whatever way you are able, and you can reach out in many different ways. Lend a helping hand or an attentive ear.

It's something wonderful to know that you brought someone's miracle, made a difference in their life, met their need. There is such a sense of freedom and joy when you can **give without expecting something in return.**

Now that is a true gift.

Be someone's miracle today!

A Servant's Heart

"Give, and it shall be given unto you" (Luke 6:38, KJV).

Let's Pray.

Father, in the name of Jesus we thank you for your still small voice that leads us daily. Amen

Plant Your Seed

FARMERS PLANT SEEDS AND receive a harvest.

In everything, there is a time to plant and a time to harvest.

Your seed is your tithe to the Lord. Give it.

Your seed is a good attitude, determination and endurance.

Your seed is not quitting.

Your seed is your faith.

Plant it, nurture it and watch it grow!

A SERVANT'S HEART

"Bring all the tithes into the storehouse,
That there may be food in My house,
And try Me now in this,"
Says the Lord of hosts,
"If I will not open for you the windows of heaven,
And pour out for you such blessing,
That there will not be room enough to receive it.
"And I will rebuke the devourer for your sakes,
So that he will not destroy the fruit for you in the field,"
Says the Lord of hosts (Malachi 3:10, NKJV).

Let's Pray.

Father, we ask you to teach us where you want us to give our time, talent and offerings daily in Jesus name. Amen

Your Picture

SEE YOURSELF STARTING TOWARDS your goal.

Keep your eye on the finish line.

Visualize your success.

Stick with your daily agenda.

Live in the moment.

Enjoy today.

Don't ever look back.

The past is history.

Keep that door closed.

Don't listen to negativity. It will break your focus.

Surround yourself with leaders, generals and positive people.

Success spreads like wildfire.

God gave us eyes in the front of our heads so that we can look to the future.

Listen forward to hear what is coming, and don't dwell on the past.

Stay the course, and you will become your picture!

A SERVANT'S HEART

"And Jesus said unto him, No man, having put his hand to the plough, and looking back, is fit for the kingdom of God" (Luke 9:62, KJV).

Let's Pray.

Father, we ask in Jesus name for your help to focus on accomplishing what you have called us to do for your glory. Amen

Schedule Your Success

BREAK DOWN YOUR GOALS into categories. Physical, Financial, Spiritual, Educational, Recreational. (**Take one day each week to play without guilt.**)

Now, under each category, define your goals.

Keep them within reach.

Setting too many goals will break your focus and confidence.

Write them down in your planner by month, week, day and then hour.

It takes thirty minutes.

You will be amazed at what you will accomplish when you follow a written plan.

Do it today. Don't let another day go by without a schedule.

Time lived without a written plan is like going on a long trip without a GPS (or map).

Stop wandering and wondering.

Take charge of your time.

You're the captain of your life!

A Servant's Heart

"And God blessed them, and God said unto them, Be fruitful, and multiply, and replenish the earth, and subdue it: **and have dominion** over the fish of the sea, and over the fowl of the air, and over every living thing that moveth upon the earth" (Genesis 1:28, KJV, emphasis mine).

Have a blessed day!

Let's Pray.

Father, in the name of Jesus teach us how to be fruitful and multiply our gifts for your kingdom purpose. Amen

Time and Talents

The Lord gave us time, gifts and talents.

It is up to us to develop each one of them.

When you take the time to invest in yourself, your life will gain confidence and momentum.

You will become an unstoppable force!

You will walk with pep in your step.

Excitement will rise within you.

Energy, excitement and confidence are the ingredients that will create your success.

A SERVANT'S HEART

"And unto one he gave five talents, to another two, and to another one; to every man according to his several ability; and straightway took his journey" (Matthew 25:15, KJV).

Let's Pray.

Father, in the name of Jesus we thank you that we will be a unstoppable force for the kingdom of God in the earth. Amen

Uncomfortable?

January 26, 2011

Don't run when you become uncomfortable in your life.

Those who won't get out of their comfort zones will not grow,

be challenged, or challenge others.

I once heard it said this way: "**Get comfortable being uncomfortable**."

Quit trying to make everything perfect.

God only uses imperfect people.

Only He is perfect.

Use the tools you have been given.

Don't compare yourself to others.

God equipped you with what you need to accomplish your heart's desires.

No more excuses.

You are a walking treasure chest.

Open yourself up and let your gifts out.

You may be an encourager.

You may be an accountant.

Whatever your gifts are,

Use them every day.

Change is possible.

Don't cling to ideas that once mattered.

Dreams and goals can change.

Don't hold onto yester-year's dreams if they don't excite you anymore.

We change.

A Servant's Heart

Nay, in all these things we are more than conquerors through him that loved us (Romans 8:37, KJV).

Let's Pray.

Father, in the name of Jesus help us to be more than conquerors through the help of the Holy Spirit. Amen

Don't Quit

NEVER, NEVER, NEVER QUIT.

The bigger the battle, the bigger the blessing.

Don't judge your pathway because things are going wrong.

Jesus told His disciples to row to the other side, and they sailed through a storm so big that it almost sunk their boat (Matthew 14:22-24). If they went through a storm while following Jesus' instructions, then you will too!

We tend to think that if we follow God's instructions, everything will go smoothly.

The opposite is true. Satan has ears too, and he will try to kill, steal and destroy what God has instructed you to do (John 10:10).

The Bible says, "Let us run with endurance the race that is set before us" (Hebrews 12:1, NKJV). This implies that there is a winner and a loser.

When you don't quit, Satan loses. There is a finish line. Be the finisher. You can do all things through Christ who strengthens you (Philippians 4:13).

One step at a time. One day at a time. One week at a time.

Don't break your focus.

A Servant's Heart

"Jesus constrained his disciples to get into a ship, and to go before him unto the other side... But the ship was now in the midst of the sea, tossed with waves" (Matthew 14:22,24, KJV).

"I can do all things through Christ Jesus who strengthens me" (Philippians 4:13, NKJV).

"The thief cometh not, but for to steal, and to kill, and to destroy: I am come that they might have life, and that they might have it more abundantly" (John 10:10, KJV).

Let's Pray.

Father, in the name of Jesus we ask for courage and confidence to keep moving forward towards our daily goals. Amen.

Toxic Thoughts

WHEN YOU BUY A cleaning product, you've probably noticed that the warning label lists the poisons in the product and what to do if you swallow it or get it in your eye. Thankfully, there is usually a remedy to the problem.

Like cleaning products, we are all vessels made for a specific purpose. We each carry gifts to develop and pour out within our lifetime. But we also carry the potential to poison our own lives as well as others.

Those poisons are created in our minds. When we entertain unhealthy thoughts, we become increasingly toxic. Like planting a garden in soil mixed with gasoline, nothing good will grow.

But there is a remedy: In order to produce a healthy outlook on our jobs, families and personal lives, we **must** control our thought lives. The Bible says that "we have the mind of Christ" (1 Corinthians 2:16, KJV). Why did God speak so specifically about this?

It is so that we can challenge ourselves to think like Jesus, whose thoughts were occupied by faith: "For with God nothing will be impossible" (Luke 1:37, NKJV).

When you choose to actively control your thoughts, you will begin to thrive. This is a way of life, to grow and become all that God created you to be. **It won't happen any other way. The only way to grow is to think differently.** It's your choice!

A Servant's Heart

I encourage you to meditate on these scriptures daily as you seek to have the mind of Christ:

"I can do all things through Christ who strengthens me" (Philippians 4:13, NKJV).

"Let this mind be in you which was also in Christ Jesus" (Philippians 2:5, NKJV).

"With men this is impossible, but with God all things are possible" (Matthew 19:26, NKJV).

"Jesus said to him, 'If you can believe, all things are possible to him who believes'" (Mark 9:23, NKJV).

Let's Pray.

Father, in the name of Jesus help us to allow the Holy Spirit to impart to us the mind of Christ. Amen

Don't Listen

Y OU WILL HEAR A lot of unbelief today.

It will resound from your television, radio and the people around you.

They will pour out doubt, negativity, fear and lack.

When you hear them talk, shut it off if you can, or walk away.

You don't serve a God of lack.

You serve the God of more than enough.

His reserves never run dry.

He is the God of blessing, healing and prosperity.

When you hear negative conversations,

You are receiving a poisonous message.

It will get into your spirit and try to change your thinking.

Your vision will become blurred.

Don't listen. Don't receive the negative report.

Whose report will you believe? I will believe the report of the Lord (Isaiah 53:1).

A Servant's Heart

"In thee, O Lord, do I put my trust: let me never be put to confusion" (Psalm 71:1, KJV).

"Be still, and know that I am God" (Psalm 46:10, KJV).

Be blessed in Him!

Let's Pray.

Father, in the name of Jesus give us a reminder every time we hear a negative report that it does not have to be that way for our lives. We will believe the report of the Lord. Amen

Vision

YOU WILL NEVER ATTAIN what you cannot see.

Until you fix your eyes, mind and spirit on your dream, you will never be able to fulfill it.

Once you **see** your goals, **lock** your focus on them with the key of **determination**.

There isn't a storm in life big enough to sink your sails.

You will move forward towards your dreams.

The desires of your heart will be filled.

But build your foundation upon the Rock of Jesus Christ.

He alone will give you the strength, endurance and peace to obtain your dreams.

Keep your eyes, ears and words in line with your path.

Keep your feet moving straight ahead.

If you get tired, rest.

If you get discouraged, pray.

If you get hurt, heal.

But keep moving forward no matter what.

Your life will become your vision!

A Servant's Heart

"Delight thyself also in the Lord; and he shall give thee the desires of thine heart" (Psalms 37:4, KJV).

"Therefore whosoever heareth these sayings of mine, and doeth them, I will liken him unto a wise man, which built is house upon a rock" (Matthew 7:24, KJV).

Be blessed in Him!

Let's Pray.

Father, in the name of Jesus help us to see the vision from the heart of the Holy Spirit for our lives. Amen

Who Is in Control?

You are what you eat.

You become what you see.

You speak what you hear.

We were created to lead, and we lead to what we follow.

Who are you listening to? The daily news? The world's system?

Who are you following? Are they going to a place where you want to end up?

If you took an impartial look at your life. Would you decide to follow you?

If not, then you need to make changes in your life today.

You lead others to the things you follow.

Be in control of your present and your future.

Be someone you would want to follow.

You were born to lead.

A SERVANT'S HEART

I have taught you in the way of wisdom;
I have led you in right paths.

When you walk, your steps will not be hindered,

And when you run, you will not stumble.

Take firm hold of instruction, do not let go;

Keep her, for she is your life (Proverbs 4:11-13, NKJV).

Let's Pray.

Father, in the name of Jesus we ask for guidance daily in our lives and that we would trust you. Amen

Listen to Others

God desires for us to listen to Him when He speaks.

He constantly desires our praise.

If God Almighty desires our attention and our praise,

How much more should we listen to and praise one other?

We were created in God's image.

We were created with a need to be heard when we speak.

We were created to be complemented.

Listen to someone today.

Praise someone, and build them up.

They will celebrate your friendship when you celebrate their worth.

A SERVANT'S HEART

Give instruction to a wise man, and he will be still wiser;
Teach a just man, and he will increase in learning.
"The fear of the Lord is the beginning of wisdom,
And the knowledge of the Holy One is understanding"
(Proverbs 9:9-10, NKJV).

Let's Pray.

Father, in the name of Jesus we will give our time and attention to those in need today. Amen

Speak to Your Mountain

Jesus said, "whosoever shall **say** unto this mountain, Be thou removed, and be thou cast into the sea; and shall not doubt in his heart, but shall believe that those things which he **saith** shall come to pass; he shall have whatsoever he **saith**" (Mark 11:23, KJV, emphasis mine).

We need to speak to our problems, not about them. It is so important to focus on and declare positive outcomes, not negative possibilities.

To every right, there is a wrong. To every up, there is a down. To every day, there is a night. To every in, there is an out.

But you must choose: What are you saying about your life— is it good or bad? What are you saying about your finances? Your family?

Jesus said that we will have what we say in faith.

Listen to yourself today. Do you want your words to come to pass? If not, then change your approach to the problem. Speak to it, and thank God for a positive outcome.

It's your choice!

Let's Pray.

Father, in the name of Jesus we ask for boldness to speak to our mountain today and command it to move in our behalf. Amen

Harvest Time

If you plant tomato seeds, you will harvest tomatoes.

If you plant grass seed, grass will grow.

If you give up your time to help someone, God will increase your time.

If you help a child, God will help your child.

If you forgive others, you will be forgiven.

God created a system of sowing and reaping.

This is the spiritual law He put in motion.

It supersedes natural conditions.

If you don't like your harvest, look at what you're planting.

Start sowing seeds for the future of your dreams.

You will live a wonderful life!

A SERVANT'S HEART

"**Give, and then** it shall be given unto you; good measure, pressed down, and shaken together, and running over, shall men give into your bosom. For with the same measure that ye mete withal it shall be measured to you again" (Luke 6:38, KJV, emphasis mine).

Let's Pray.

Father, in the name of Jesus we will plant our seed today knowing we will receive a harvest in due time. Amen

Breakthrough

DO YOU DESIRE MORE FOR your life than what you currently have? Do you see visions of your dreams fulfilled? Don't believe the lie that your dreams are mere fantasies, and that you're not one of the chosen ones who are fortunate enough to live their dreams.

Remember, everything that you need to become all that you want to be is already inside of you. The power is untapped, lying asleep, but **it is there**.

God Almighty breathed **His** own breath into you and made you in His image. You are a son or daughter of the most high God. His DNA and genes are the fibers of your being.

Stop and think about that for a moment. Just as your children have your blood running through their veins and are made in your image, so it is with you and the Lord.

The power of the Holy Spirit lives within you. All you have to do is tap in. Ask for His presence, wisdom, determination.

When a runner is working towards a goal, he follows the "SAID" principle: *Specific Adaption to Imposed Demands*. When he hits a wall, he mentally reaches inward and draws the strength to run further. He forces his body to *specifically adapt* to his *demand*.

His body screams, "No! I can't. I'm tired!" But the runner replies, "Oh yes you can, and you will!" And his body demolishes the wall. The next time he runs that same distance, the demand will not be as strong because he has already broken through that wall.

Like that runner, when you push towards your dreams and goals, your thoughts might turn against you, reminding you that you're not smart or talented enough to succeed, or that you don't have the money. You have to say back to yourself, "I can. I have the Lord to help me, and He will lead me to people who know how to do what I can't. He will show me the way."

Trust God's faithfulness, and you will break through! Don't quit!

Let's Pray.

Father, in the name of Jesus we thank you that we are filled with your DNA. We are the children of God. Amen

Command and Demand

W**HETHER OR NOT THEY** realize it, all athletes understand the SAID principle, *Specific Adaption to Imposed Demands.* They all *specifically* make their bodies *adapt* to the *demands* that they *impose* upon their muscles. When they encourage themselves, they are able to go further. This is a godly principle.

"In the beginning… **God SAID,** Let there be light: and there was light" (Genesis 1:1,3, KJV, emphasis mine).

With His words, God Himself *specifically imposed* a *demand* upon light to come into existence. He saw what He wanted, spoke it with full confidence in His power, and darkness bowed its knee.

Then God created us in His image to follow His example. We can *specifically demand* that the natural world conform to God's supernatural truth, for He designed the world to *adapt* to the *demands* we *impose.* "[F]ill the earth and subdue it; have dominion" (Genesis 1:28, NKJV). If we seek His will and find comfort in His presence, then we, too, will accomplish anything we set our minds to.

When we speak with determination and faith in an almighty God, our difficult circumstance will bow its knee. It may be school, a job, healing or a broken relationship, but whatever it is, reach within yourself, "for greater is he that is **in** you, than he that is in the world" (1 John 4:4, KJV, emphasis mine).

Use God's SAID principle; your words are your weapon! You can, you will, you win! You can do it!

A Servant's Heart

"Let this mind be in you which was also in Christ Jesus" (Philippians 2:5, KJV).

"[W]hosoever shall… believe that those things which he saith shall come to pass; he shall have whatsoever he saith" (Mark 11:23, KJV).

"He that walketh with wise men shall be wise: but a companion of fools shall be destroyed" (Proverbs 13:20, KJV).

Let's Pray.

Father, we ask the Holy Spirit to teach us how to encourage ourselves as King David did in the book of Psalm's in Jesus name. Amen

Get the Picture?

ARENTS OFTEN "GROUND" THEIR children as a form of punishment. They proceed to state what the child cannot do for the next month, and end by saying, "Get the picture?"

Like that example, we have each heard the words that people have spoken over us as children and adults, and we develop mental images of ourselves accordingly— who we are, and who we can never be.

If you have been unfortunate in this area and people have spoken negatively of you, then you might have an untrue, unhealthy self-image. You have taken their words into a darkroom within your heart and developed a negative picture.

But you can change the way you see yourself the same way: with words!

Surround yourself with people who fly like eagles— who take positive actions to move forward and encourage each other. People who are leaders in their fields, and who have a positive disposition. Listen to encouraging speakers. Read encouraging books.

You must hear the words first, and then you will develop a new mental picture of yourself and your future.

You are equipped to accomplish your dreams. Why else do you think you have those dreams?

You are strong enough, and God will place the right people along your path to help you. He is the One who gave you the desires of your heart. He wants you to fulfill your calling, and He said that with Him, **nothing is impossible**.

Get the picture?

A Servant's Heart

"For with God nothing shall be impossible" (Luke 1:37, KJV).

Let's Pray.

Father, in the name of Jesus we come to you for help. We give our old hurts and wounds over to you. We allow you to rebuild us from the inside out. Amen

Opportunity

I ONCE HEARD SOMEONE SAY, "When opportunity knocks, open the door." I say, opportunity knocks every waking hour of the day!

In the kingdom of God, opportunity is the **chance to sow a seed**. And when you plant a seed, it grows.

You are a walking bag of seeds. Everything that you do sows a seed that you will eventually harvest. Sow kindness into the cashier at the supermarket, give an extra dollar to the charity outside the door, help your next-door neighbor, forgive someone. Everything you do today is a seed. Plant good things!

God only gives to those who give willingly. How can you receive from Him if your hand is closed? To those who give, more will be given. This is God's system.

Opportunity only happens when you make it happen!

Don't wait for something or someone to come to you. Be the open door! Plant the seed! Today is an open door for opportunity. Make it happen.

A SERVANT'S HEART

And if thou draw out thy soul to the hungry, and satisfy the afflicted soul; then shall thy light rise in obscurity, and thy darkness be as the noon day:

And the Lord shall guide thee continually, and satisfy thy soul in drought, and make fat thy bones: and thou shalt be like a watered garden, like a spring of water, whose waters fail not (Isaiah 58:10-11, KJV).

Let's Pray.

Father, we ask the Holy Spirit for help to give us the strength to give more of our selves as we grow in your kingdom in Jesus name. Amen

The Mood

 A NICE DINNER, CANDLELIGHT AND soft music create a romantic atmosphere for two people to connect intimately.

A high school rally before a football game creates an energetic atmosphere to help the team win.

Creating atmospheres is important for reaching goals. We each carry an atmosphere or mood about us every day.

Do you remember Charlie Brown's friend, Pig Pen, from the *Peanuts* comics? He was surrounded by a swirling cloud of dirt which followed him wherever he walked. Pig Pen is a good illustration of the atmosphere our moods create as we journey through life.

What hovers around you every day? When your family comes home, do they dread the negativity you put out? Do gray clouds cast shadows wherever you walk?

When your name is mentioned, a general picture of you comes to the minds of the people who know you. You are a walking atmosphere, a carrier of influence. What environment are you creating for people on a daily basis?

You are a mood.

You have the power to radiate joy. You can laugh and thrive. You have the ability to be the sunshine in someone's dark moment. Or, you can cast darkness over someone's sunny day. What do you want to be known for?

Be responsible for your attitude, your mood, your atmosphere. Don't succumb to angry blow-ups just because you're under pressure. Be responsible for the power that you have been given to take charge of the atmosphere you create for others.

A SERVANT'S HEART

"A merry heart doeth good like a medicine: but a broken spirit drieth the bones" (Proverbs 17:22, KJV).

Let's Pray.

Father, we ask for courage to grow from selfishness to mature people in your sight. That we would allow the Holy Spirit to correct us when we are negative in Jesus name. Amen

Obstacles

Overcomers are people who refuse to focus on their problems.

It's not that the problems aren't there.

They see the obstacles, but they think differently about them.

Others see potential failures, but they see opportunities for God's glory.

Stop focusing on the reasons why you can't overcome.

Visualize your success in that area.

You must start using visualization as a tool.

Tools are the means by which you can accomplish a task.

If you want to put together a bike, you pick up a wrench and a screwdriver.

You consistently reference a picture of the finished bike.

A few hours later, voila! You have a bike that looks like the picture.

In the same way, **visualization is necessary a tool**.

Allow yourself to dream.

See yourself achieving your goal.

Let go of worry and doubt.

Take one simple step at a time in the direction of your dream.

One day, you will look back a say, "Voila! I did it!"

You must, you will, and you can!

A SERVANT'S HEART

"For who hath despised the day of small things?" (Zechariah 4:10, KJV).

Let's Pray.

Father, we thank you for the power you gave us to stand up to obstacles in our lives in Jesus name. Amen

Training

HAVE YOU EVER WATCHED a documentary or read about a rescue operation? For example, envision a group of inexperienced hiker lost in a snow storm high in a mountainous wilderness. They feel trapped and are in total disarray. It all seems like a nightmare that is only made worse by the fear that plagues their thoughts like the winds of a hurricane. The hopelessness that takes over their minds is actually more dangerous than their situation.

But a rescue team is unleashed into the same treacherous situation, and they approach the storm with calm minds and confidence. Their strength seems to overpower the natural forces against them. They look into the eye of the storm as if to say, "We are here now, so back off while we rescue these people!" And they do!

Afterwards, the victims are traumatized and severely exhausted by the event, while the rescue team is just a little winded. They experienced the same awful elements, but one group is in shock, and the other is fine. Why? Because of one word: Training. The rescuers spend more time in training than they do on rescue missions so that, when their skills are needed, they are ready!

In the same way, when things go wrong in our lives and a storm hits, we need to be prepared with the proper training.

"How do I train?" you ask? You pray, trust God and commit to faith. Take time to rest, take in good nutrition and exercise every day—physically and spiritually. Learn how to trust the Lord with your every need.

When you allow God to train you, you will be ready to handle any problem, no matter how unexpected. This doesn't mean that your challenges won't be tough, but instead of coming out all busted up and depressed, you will look into the eye of the storm and say, "Back off, I'm coming through!"

And you will! Pray, trust and commit!

A SERVANT'S HEART

"**Watch** ye and **pray**, lest ye enter into temptation. The spirit truly is ready, but the flesh is weak" (Mark 14:38, KJV).

Let's Pray.

Father, in the name of Jesus we will stay in your presence and allow the Holy Spirit to fight the good fight of faith through us. Amen

Vengeance Is Mine!

WE HAVE ALL HEARD it said, "Treat others as you would want to be treated" (see Luke 6:31). But we inevitably discover that sometimes when we treat others well, they don't return the kindness. Our hearts can easily become calloused against these hurts, and our attitudes suffer.

As life goes on, pride tempts us to take it upon ourselves to give people what they deserve, instead of offering them free grace. But the Word of God says, "Vengeance is mine; I will repay, saith the Lord" (Romans 12:19, KJV).

We are to follow Christ's example, who said that we should not forgive someone seven times, but "seventy times seven" (Matthew 18:22, KJV). Four hundred ninety times is a lot of unrequited, undeserved forgiveness. We are to walk in love at all times.

You may wonder why God can seek vengeance if we cannot. It is because God's anger is righteous. The difference between our bad attitudes and His vengeance is based on truth and integrity. God sees everyone in their mothers' wombs; He knows everything about them. The person who is a thorn to you may have had a very hard time in life. You cannot possibly see the whole picture.

God's vengeance is not against one person; it is against Satan— the one who hurts both you and them. Satan is the true culprit of every evil. God's plan is to punish him and rescue us. He needs us to walk with patience and love for others while He works out the plan of attack against our real enemy.

But if you take matters into your own hands, God can't work for your good or the good of those you punish. You will bind yourself up with jealousy, hate and negativity. Let go of your plan, and let the God of justice take over. He knows how to deliver you, and He will!

A SERVANT'S HEART

The Spirit of the Lord is upon me, because he hath anointed me to preach the gospel to the poor; he hath sent me to heal the brokenhearted, to preach deliverance to the captives, and recovering of sight to the blind, to set at liberty them that are bruised,

To preach the acceptable year of the Lord (Luke 4:18-19, KJV).

Ye have heard that it hath been said, An **eye for an eye**, and a tooth for a tooth: But I say unto you, That ye resist not evil: but whosoever shall smite thee on thy right cheek, turn to him the other also (Matthew 5:38-39, KJV).

Let's Pray.

Father, in the name of Jesus we forgive others just as you have forgiven us. Amen

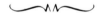

Stuck in the Mud

Have you ever gotten your car stuck in the mud? No matter how many times you press on the gas pedal, your tires spin and sink deeper. In the same way, we can get stuck in our lives. Instead of growing and moving forward, we stay in the same place year after year.

Being stuck in your life is a very serious situation.

You have to confront yourself, look deep into your heart and ask tough questions, like, "Why am I in this place? Why can't I move on?" Then, just as importantly, you have to be willing to hear the truth. When we ask heartfelt questions, the Lord opens our eyes to the answers.

If we have experienced trauma, disappointment or hurt earlier in our lives, it is easy to respond to new hurts out of habit. Meaning, we respond to today's issues the same way we responded when we were children or young adults. This happens because we never healed properly then, but life moved forward anyway.

We handle issues with fear, anger and manipulation, which we take out on the people who care most about us. And we become stagnant inside, never growing, like a tulip bulb in the ground that waits for spring but never comes up. So much potential lies dormant within us, but we are unable to move forward because of yesterday's issues.

You may not even recognize this within yourself, but if you are not growing or moving forward **with great joy and peace, wanting the same for everyone else**, then the chances are high that you are stuck in the mud.

Be courageous and confront yourself. This is not the time to look back and point the finger at someone else. This is about **you**! Quit blaming others and staying underground like a tulip bulb. Confront, let go and grow. God has blessed you with gifts, and you can bless Him by using what He gave you.

A SERVANT'S HEART

"You hypocrite, first take the plank out of your own eye, and then you will see clearly to remove the speck from your brother's eye" (Matthew 7:5, NIV).

Let's Pray.

Father, in the name of Jesus we ask for help daily to confront our inner man with what needs to change so we can live the lives we truly desire. Amen

Can I Still Help?

HAVE YOU EVER GONE on a road trip and found yourself lost, having made a wrong turn or missed an exit? Then you have to turn around and go all the way back to get on the right track. Finally, you reach your destination; you're late, but you made it.

Later, if someone asked you for directions to the same place, would you help them or say, "I can't give you directions because I made a wrong turn and had to go back to find the right road"? You would probably say, "Sure," and proceed to guide them based on the knowledge you gained from your mistake.

In the same way, through life's journeys, we make mistakes and bad decisions, and get lost along the way. **And then we get back on the right track and keep moving forward.**

Many Christians are so easily convinced of the lie that God cannot use them because they have made too many mistakes. We slip into a mode of sadness, guilt and even depression, allowing our gifts to become dormant.

This is as silly as the example about not helping someone just because you got lost. We have to start recognizing the bag of tricks the enemy uses to corner us. Satan wants you to believe that your bad choices have removed you from God's grace and purpose. He specifically doesn't want you to draw from your past experiences *because* they will help others.

You must defeat that lie no matter what. No matter what! The Lord will always use you no matter what you are going through or where you end up.

Do not stop helping others. Do not stop growing. Do not stop loving and sharing yourself. Do not stop teaching, preaching, singing, dancing, painting and working! We need you!

A Servant's Heart

"Greater love hath no man than this, that a man lay down his life for his friends" (John 15:13, KJV).

Let's Pray.

Father, in the name of Jesus we will allow the Holy Spirit to use us in the kingdom of God as you want to. Amen

Habits

A BABY IS A MIRACLE from God, but the miracle won't take place before the mothers first endures labor. In the same way, your dreams and goals will never transpire if you do not first pursue them.

Time, determination and patience are some very important keys to achieving your goals. Without them, you will become tired and discouraged, and quit.

Focus, pray and commit to whatever you want to go after in life. You will have to spend some days fighting and sweating through adversity. You will have to create good habits. Your priorities will have to change to line up with your vision. Success must become your daily pursuit.

The only reason you are not living the life you want to live is that you are not **choosing** to take the steps to get there.

Are you pursuing the life that you really want? If not, stop and change your direction.

A SERVANT'S HEART

"Be not deceived; God is not mocked: for whatsoever a man soweth, that shall he also reap" (Galatians 6:7, KJV).

Let's Pray.

Father, in the name of Jesus we allow the Lord to confront us when we fall back into bad daily habits. Amen

Paying the Price

WHILE I WAS OUT shopping once, I looked at the price tag on the merchandise and heard a voice clearly whisper to my heart, "Are you willing to pay the price?"

I knew that the Holy Spirit was speaking to me, and I thought to myself, "I would if I thought it was worth it."

I knew that God's question had nothing to do with the merchandise at the store, but that this was a lifelong question.

We admire those who live successfully and confidently. They seem to bulldoze through issues, and they always come through smiling. They not only come out stronger, but more content. They seem to look fear in the eyes and say, "There isn't room for the two of us here," and fear packs it bags and makes a run for it.

You wonder to yourself, *How can they do this?*

They are willing to pay the price to have what they want in life.

There is always a cost to having something or someone in your life. If you don't want to pay the price for your dream, then where will you end up? Will you find yourself aging alone? Will you live with regret?

Yes, there is a price to pay, and it is high, but the price you will pay for not confronting yourself and choosing to grow is much greater.

Don't find yourself living in regret at the end of your life. Think on these things carefully. Pay the price now so you won't pay it later!

A SERVANT'S HEART

"For Christ also hath once suffered for sins, the just for the unjust, that he might bring us to God, being put to death in the flesh, but quickened by the Spirit" (1 Peter 3:18, KJV).

Let's Pray.

Father, in the name of Jesus we make a decision today to pay the price that is takes to move forward in our life and we ask for your help. Amen

What about Love?

WE HAVE ALWAYS LIVED in a world filled with both good and evil, but lately things seem to be spinning out of control. Human behavior appears to be regressing towards a more barbaric state. It is almost as if the conscience of humanity has been severed from the heart of God completely. What has happened to love?

Now take an introspective look. Are you choosing the right behavior in your everyday life? It may seem less clear once you examine your own actions. After all, God would understand the reasons why we treat people the way we do. Surely He would agree with our reasoning. Friendship, love, honor and commitment are definitely good things, but only if they bring *us* the best possible outcome, right?

But then, there is Jesus. He gave His word that He would come to Earth and pour out His life for mankind. And Jesus also poured His life into men, namely His twelve disciples, as He walked the Earth. He spent hundreds of hours teaching them. He preached to thousands of people and healed the sick. **He gave all of Himself for years.**

Then, when everyone thought He was done, He died and shed His blood for us. He stood up for us in the face of Satan and his demons, and He would not let us go. He gave us honor, though we spat on Him and jeered at Him.

But why? He did this because He had asked Himself the same question: *What about love?*

And I will leave you with this thought: Where is our love? If we cannot show it in simple ways, then how can we expect to give in more difficult times?

Is love stopped by your pocketbook or your bottom line? Does your love have conditions?

Love is an action, not an emotion.

A SERVANT'S HEART

"By this we know love, **because He laid down His life** for us. And we also ought to **lay down our lives** for the brethren" (1 John 3:16, NKJV, emphasis mine).

Let's Pray.

Father, in the name of Jesus we ask for impartation of your love to help us love others the way you want us to love them. Amen

Visions Dancing in My Head

REMEMBER WHEN YOU WERE a small child, how you longed for winter to come? You would stand inside with your nose pressed against the cold window, thinking, "If only it would snow! Oh, when will it come? When it snows, I will be the happiest kid ever!" If you stared at the sky long enough, you were sure that the snow would fall.

Then you would pull on your rubber boots and mittens, run outside, throw yourself into the biggest snow drift you could find, and flail your arms and legs back and forth into the shape of an angel, sticking out your tongue to catch the snowflakes as they fell.

We adults are similar, except that we don't anxiously press our noses against windows or stare expectantly into the sky. We believe our happiness lies in pay raises, or we think to ourselves, "If someone would only do this one thing for me, then I will be the most content person ever!"

If only, if only, if only, then I will be truly happy.

I ask you, Deep down, **do you really believe that?** If it were true, wouldn't you be happy by now?

The only thing, the only way, the only one who can bring you true happiness is **Jesus.**

Are you not tired of searching and wondering if you will ever be able to fill that void within your soul, or have you come to believe that you will always have that emptiness inside of you?

Visions dancing in your head are a fine thing, and they should always be there, but even when they are fulfilled, they can't complete you. The only thing that will fulfill your heart's desires is the love you receive by accepting Jesus into your heart.

Then, no matter where you are, what you have or who you are with, you will be full of unending joy, peace and contentment.

There isn't anything like it!

A SERVANT'S HEART

Let's Pray.

Father, in the name of Jesus we ask and thank you for your peace and contentment in our hearts so we can be a blessing to those all around us. Amen

Signs Change You

COMPANIES SPEND MILLIONS OF dollars each year creating and maintaining billboards along major highways. By posting giant pictures of juicy hamburgers and refreshing beverages, advertisers have discovered that they can make you hungry or thirsty enough to pull off to their franchise at the next exit. They know that if they catch a quick glance of your sight as you drive, they can influence you enough to spend money on their products.

That is the power of images!

And if an advertiser can create hunger in your stomach within a split second, then you can certainly develop a hunger for your goals by focusing on them. Whether you want a better home, car or boat; or you want to become a better musician, athlete, author or artist, fix your gaze upon your goal.

Cut out pictures and find scriptures in the Bible that encourage you and build your faith. Write the scriptures and goals underneath the pictures, and put them in your bathroom, kitchen, bedroom, office and car.

God is for you and your goals. He wants you to obtain your dreams— in fact, He will help you.

What you see on a daily basis affects you. If think this is silly, then you might want to tell all the advertisers to tear their billboards down and stop spending billions of dollars on commercials. They would laugh and say you are silly!

They would also know in a moment that you will have a harder time reaching your goals than they will.

It is a choice! Go for it!

A Servant's Heart

"Mine eye affecteth mine heart" (Lamentations 3:51, KJV).

Let's Pray.

Father, in the name of Jesus as we read your word we believe we will be filled with your divine perception and joy. Amen.

Complainers

You will hear a lot of complaining today. See it for what it is: unbelief!

If you open yourself up to this way of thinking, it will abort your visions and goals.

Do not participate. Recognize the negative spirit that poisons every conversation, and confront it with truth and hope when appropriate. If not, it may be best to leave the room.

Take charge of whom and what you listen to.

A Servant's Heart

"And when the people complained, it displeased the Lord: and the Lord heard it; and his anger was kindled; and the fire of the Lord burnt among them, and consumed them that were in the uttermost parts of the camp" (Numbers 11:1).

Let's Pray.

Father, help us from allowing depression from entering into our hearts, allowing toxic thoughts to be our direction. We give our future to you and trust you. Amen

Centerpiece

A WELL DECORATED ROOM HAS a way of making you feel calm, as if your body was saying, *Ahhh, this is nice.* Your eyes admire the decor, and you wish they were camera lenses so that you could, remember everything exactly, in hopes that you will be able to create this same setting in your own home.

Then you notice the centerpiece of the room, and how the atmosphere has been entirely orchestrated around it. It seems to stand tall and proud, opening wide its arms and saying, "Look at the colors of this room, the light flowing in through the windows and the paintings on the walls. Look at all that I have inspired."

And the centerpiece is right! The paintings on the walls, the rugs that hug the floors, and the way light streams through the curtains like a gentle brook all work together because they were designed from the centerpiece, and it ties them together. Without it, none of it would work. It would just be a room with a rug by the door and a picture on the wall.

Our lives are much like the well decorated room centered around one focal point. We were created by the Great Designer, and we are made up of many different parts. We are spiritual, physical, emotional and intellectual human beings with various gifts and talents. Each of those parts are wonderful, but without a centerpiece connecting them, they remain just that: parts.

When Jesus is the Centerpiece of our hearts and the Connector of our lives, all that is within us flows out from His inspiration. Our emotions are in perfect balance with our minds. Our every gift and talent connects so beautifully through Him. Prosperity, peace and joy pour out so stunningly that people want to know us better.

Only God's indwelling presence has the power to unlock your great capacity and share it with the world.

So, if you feel like you are full of great gifts and ideas, but you are not accomplishing anything with them, then connect yourself to your Centerpiece and watch yourself grow!

A Servant's Heart

"But I am like a green olive tree in the house of God; I trust in and confidently rely on the loving-kindness and the mercy of God forever and ever" (Psalm 52:8).

Let's Pray.

Father, we ask Jesus to become our tree of life. We need Him to be our centerpiece in Jesus name. Amen

Dignity

JOHN THE BAPTIST WAS called by God to prepare the way for Jesus. He faithfully answered that call and went into the dusty wilderness of Judea, boldly proclaiming the coming of the One whose sandal strap he was "not worthy to loose" (Luke 3:16, NKJV).

John's voice rang through the countryside, like a bell in a tower on a quiet night, saying, "Repent, for the kingdom of heaven is at hand!" (Matthew 3:2, NKJV). And, "[H]e shall baptize you with the Holy Ghost, and with fire" (Matthew 3:11, KJV).

The Pharisees, scribes and Sadducees— whom we might compare to wealthy, hypocritical pastors, priests and Christians who use religion to preserve their lavish lifestyles— were disgusted with this man who called himself a messenger from God!

Admittedly, John wasn't much to look at. He was filthy from the long, hot days in the desert, and his beard was unkempt. He may not even have been an especially skilled speaker. The religious leaders crossed their arms and looked down at him, while his voice thundered into the hearts of men who were searching for something to fill their empty lives, and finding it in his message.

There was also David, the second king of Israel— a man whom God Himself called, "**a man after his own heart**" (1 Samuel 13:14, KJV, emphasis mine). God told His prophet, Samuel, to go to Jesse's house and anoint one of his sons to be the king of Israel. He said, "**Do not look at his appearance or at his physical stature… For the Lord does not see**

as man sees; for man looks at the outward appearance, but the Lord looks at the heart" (1 Samuel 16:7, NKJV, emphasis mine).

David was his father's eighth and youngest son, and Jesse didn't even bother to call him inside for consideration with the rest. David was even the prophet's last choice, but still, he was the one God chose. The Holy Spirit anointed David as a king and a prophet because he loved his heart.

The Lord and David were extremely close, though David faced numerous battles in his life. His kids rebelled, and he had an affair with the wife of one of his best generals. David went so far as to kill the man just to get away with his sin.

David paid a high price for his mistakes, but he repented before his God, and God loved him through the pain. He never turned away. David's life was not easy, but through it all, he lived to glorify God. He never took his eyes off of Him, and he kept his humility and his zeal for the house of the Lord. As a result, the Son of God was called, "the Son of David" (see Matthew 21:9).

God still works through us to accomplish His redemptive purpose. He is not looking for Christian dignity— Those who are ashamed of their testimonies, comfortable in their rituals and unwilling to unfold their arms. He is looking for people who will accomplish **His purpose no matter what they go through**. He will use those who remain undignified and full of compassion for people. God will fulfill His plan through those who are willing.

Dignity or Christianity? It is your choice!

A SERVANT'S HEART

Let's Pray.

Father, in the name of Jesus we ask for a willing heart to please you. Amen.

Go ahead and Turn Your Back!

"I WILL NEVER TURN MY back on you!" This saying expresses a binding love between people that will keep them together through life's journey, no matter what comes their way.

We are taught to love, respect and treat people the way we want to be treated, and that we should serve others without expecting anything in return. We are told that this is the right thing to do and the right way to live.

We begin our journeys with this truth in our hearts, but as time goes on, we grow weary. The arrows of life pierce our hearts with disappointment and cause us to forget our great purpose. We start to withdraw and think about how much we have done for others. We retreat within ourselves and pity our wounds as if life were a tragic movie. We become bitter and tired, practically shaking our fists toward Heaven in anger and regret. "I've given so much, and look where I am now!"

Jesus came to the Earth at Heaven's command: *Give Yourself to the world and open Your hand. Give them life, healing and hope.* He fed the crowds and healed the sick and dead. His feet were sore, and His voice was strained. He loved them, and He wept for them. And then what did He get? The world turned on Him, yelling, "Crucify Him!" (Mark 15:13, NKJV).

But Jesus didn't pity His tragic circumstance. He turned His back to them so that they could take a whip made with nine leather sashes, each tied up with iron nails. Every time that whip sunk into His flesh and was ripped out again, it tore gaping wounds. Jesus endured 40 of these unimaginable lashes for you and me. His heart cried out to His Heavenly Father, "forgive **them**, for they do not know what they do" (Luke 23:34, NKJV)!

Jesus died for us, and He lived with no regret. He followed God's purpose for His life, and He wants you to return to God's purpose for yours. It is time for you to carry your cross and turn your back for those who God has put in your life, for you to practice the amazing love of Christ and live as a testimony of His grace, even for those who hurt you. We are to be like Jesus and imitate His life and love, so we must turn our backs and endure the unkindness of this world and give to them love in return.

A Servant's Heart

But He was wounded for our transgressions, He was bruised for our iniquities; The chastisement for our peace was upon Him, And by **His stripes** we are healed" (Isaiah 53:5, NKJV, emphasis mine).

Let's Pray.

Father, in the name of Jesus we ask for your help and ability to live our lives without regret. We want to become all that you called us to be. Amen

Keep Your Eyes on the Road

DO YOU WONDER WHY you are not obtaining your goals? Do you feel overwhelmed?

That is probably because you have taken your eyes off of the next step. If you look too far ahead, then your plans will crash and burn. If you look back, you will get lost in your past. You have to focus your attention on today's goals because today is the only day you can actively control.

What needs to be addressed today in order to move you towards accomplishing your goal tomorrow? Today is the day you take action!

Make a list of priorities, and gradually scratch off everything you accomplish day by day, until you have completed everything you wrote down.

This is the way to your pot of gold at the end of the rainbow. These are the keys to success!

You can do it!

A SERVANT'S HEART

Let's Pray.

Father, in the name of Jesus we thank you for empowering us to grow and dominate our sphere of influence. Amen

What Is Hope?

HAVE YOU EVER LIT a match in a dark room?

Have you ever felt a warm sunray on a cold, snowy day?

That is what hope is. **It is a change!**

Hope is believing that where you are now is not where you will be tomorrow.

Hope is the engine of your faith.

Without hope, you will never expect anything greater than what you have.

You will end up depressed, lonely and desolate, like a third world country wrought with pain and hunger, with no foreseeable way out.

If you're losing hope, then you have taken your eyes off of the Lord and fixed them on your issues. All you see is the situation.

Remember, what you think about is what you will eventually believe. Focus your eyes and mind back on the Word of God. Think about God's great goodness.

You cannot afford to lose the **power** of hope. It is the secret of the Lord!

> **"For I know the plans I have for you,"** declares the Lord, **"plans to prosper you and not to harm you, plans to give you hope and a future.** Then you will call on me and come and pray to me, and I will listen to you. You will seek me and find me when you seek me with all your heart" (Jeremiah 29:11-13, NIV, emphasis mine).

A Servant's Heart

Let's Pray.

Father, in the name of Jesus we will seek you with all of our heart. Amen.

Life Changes

ONE THING THAT IS certain from the day you are born is that your life will continually go through some kind of change. Your age and appearance will change. Your knowledge will change. The people in your life will change. The weather will change as the seasons change.

So I ask you this question: Why are you surprised that you are going through change today?

This is life; it does not stay the same. It never has, and it never will.

However, **we are to respond to change, not react to it.** We should not follow our emotions through life as if they are in charge. We are to take the lead and allow our emotions to follow. If you allow your emotions to take the reins, you will end up on an unpredictable rollercoaster.

Emotions have a wonderful purpose, but they can be deadly if they become the captain of your ship. Ultimately, they will either drive you into the rocks or lose you out at sea.

Your life will always be changing. Set goals, and firmly decide not to take your eyes off of them. Your emotions may kick and scream at times, and that is okay. They will follow you like a child; that is the way it is supposed to be.

Respond to life's changes; do not react to them. As the captain of your ship, you will get to where you want to go!

You can do it.

A SERVANT'S HEART

Even the youths shall faint and be weary, and the young men shall utterly fall:

But they that wait upon the Lord shall renew their strength; they shall mount up with wings as eagles; they shall run, and not be weary; and they shall walk, and not faint (Isaiah 40:30-31, KJV).

Let's Pray.

Father, we need your ability to handle change on a daily base. We need your courage and peace to move forward in Jesus name. Amen

Overcoming

BACK IN THE DAY when Jesus walked the Earth, following the Father's call on His life, He must have felt isolated and alone. He walked with His closest friends, but He poured Himself out for others every day.

One day, as they stopped to rest, Jesus asked His disciples a question to see where they were in their understanding of what He had taught them: "Who do people say I am?" (Mark 8:27, NIV).

They muttered various answers, but Jesus was longing for someone to realize the one true answer. *Do they know how much I long for them to be inside My heart to feel the separation I feel as I walk out this calling alone?*

And then He heard an answer that was like music to His ears or a shot of cortisone in His veins, and His spirits were lifted. Peter said, "You are the Christ, the Son of the living God" (Matthew 16:16, NKJV).

And Jesus replied, "Blessed are you, Simon son of Jonah, for this was not revealed to you by flesh and blood, but by my Father in heaven. And I tell you that you are Peter, and on this rock I will build my church, and the gates of Hades will not overcome it" (Matthew 16:17-18, NIV).

Finally, Jesus knew that His Father had broken through the darkness in the hearts of men. The truth had penetrated the veils that Satan had draped over the minds of men long ago. Man once again connected to his original position with God, where he could see and hear from the kingdom of Heaven. What a moment and what a day!

Jesus made a clear and powerful annotation that day. He spoke precisely chosen words into the heavens and the Earth forever: "UPON THIS ROCK I WILL BUILD MY CHURCH; AND THE GATES OF HELL WILL NOT PREVAIL AGAINST IT" (Matthew 16:17-18, KJV).

Jesus overcame! Jesus won because He didn't quit as He traveled and preached and taught the truth: "It's not over! God loves you. Don't quit. I'm here!"

Don't quit, keep your dreams and pursue your goals. It is not over! He is here!

The gates of Hell cannot stop you!

A SERVANT'S HEART

Let's Pray.

Father, we thank you for your angels that will go before us preparing our steps ahead as we continually move through our journey in this life time, in Jesus name. Amen

Salvation Prayer:

Pray this prayer with me. "Oh Father in Heaven, I believe with all of my heart that Jesus has been raised from the dead. I believe your Word, and I repent of my sin. Come into my heart, Lord Jesus. I receive my forgiveness. I receive salvation. Fill me with Your Spirit, in Jesus' name.

Amen."

I encourage you to read this devotional many times in your life and allow the Holy Spirit to always perform his work in and through you.

Thank you,

In His Love,

Lori

References used in book

Faith and Confession –Charles Capps, copyright 1987

Seeds of Wisdom-Mike Murdock, Copyright 1993

Who switched off MY Brain, Dr. Caroline Leaf, Copyright 2007

© 2012 Merriam-Webster, Incorporated

Pastor Joel A. Brooks, Jr.
Senior Pastor - Christian Life Center
1225 W. Paterson
Kalamazoo, MI 49007
www.clcglobal.org

CPSIA information can be obtained at www.ICGtesting.com
Printed in the USA
BVOW041801180313

315818BV00002B/6/P

9 781449 779368